P9-CAN-899

SAUCELITO-AUALITO

Legends and tales of a changing town

George Hoffman

A Woodward Book

Drawings by Bill Dempster

Composition by Shirl Bolton

Special thanks to Sol and Bea Cohen
whose encouragement made the book possible.

Copyright 1976 by George Hoffman

All rights reserved
including the right of reproduction
in whole or in part in any form.

A Woodward Book
Box 773
Corte Madera, Ca.
94925

ISBN 0-916028-02-x
Library of Congress Catalog Card Number 76-716

AUTHOR'S NOTE

Herewith are some tales of people, places and events that helped make Sausalito what it was B.C. (Before Commercialization) and left it like it is. The period covers the 1940s, '50s and '60s, with a few before-and-after accounts for continuity.

The book is dedicated to the people who will say they could have done better but haven't. The invitation is open to them to try. There will be criticisms of the book, but none as harsh as my own. Within my own limits and knowing my capacity and ability, I have done my best and enjoyed doing it.

This is not a historical book nor intended to be. It's doubtful that serious historians would learn of the persons mentioned in these pages, or believe that the ripples they made had anything to do with shaping Sausalito. Your author would disagree. The smallest grape in the vineyard contributes to the wine. Everyone who lived in Sausalito had a part in its past which in some small way influenced its future, and that makes history.

Some of the names in these pages represent persons living and dead, but most of the characters are fictitious. In many cases I have invented people to meet the situation and sometimes twisted the scene to be consistent with the character. An author is expected to do that, and he must if he is fantasizing as I did. Cooks do it when they attempt to achieve a certain flavor; adding a spice or two which they think will bring out the best in the ingredients. It is not expected that everyone will like the flavor.

Many of the events in the book did happen, some did not. I started to write a history but soon discovered that the facts were so boring that I lost interest. Some events had to be expanded and some parts deleted to fit and make sense. Many people will recognize events and wonder why I didn't tell it like it was. That has been answered.

Apologies are in order to the people who contributed to Sausalito but who are not mentioned in these pages and should have been.

The book could have been written in two words, and was; the title. It is what has happened to Sausalito. The words in the text bridge the gap between.

I wish to say that I have been extremely careful not to ridicule or embarrass anyone, and hope I have succeeded. My hope is that anyone who is displeased will accept my most humble apologies.

Sausalito is an enigma. As such, anyone asserting that he knows the answers to the inexplicable has more confidence in himself than respect for illusions. Your author is humbled by mystery and stands in awe at the intangible. These pages show that there are no simple answers.

For Mary

We sit lotus-wise
On our roof, while the brown flood
Swirls slowly below.

Now Moments
Mary Hoffman

1

Between the period when Mexico controlled California and the year 1850, when the territory became a state of the union, a few white settlers had discovered Saucelito and were busy making a town out of it. Why they came before any shops were built is not known. But what is known hasn't been written in any authoritative books. It's as if archivists wish to protect proud citizens who would just as soon forget the disreputable beginning. There have been many historical facts written and rewritten about some of the early settlers and they are all credible accounts as far as they go. Men like John Reed and John Richardson were worth writing about. And don't forget the conquistadors. They came in for a great deal of accounting when space needed filling up or a date couldn't be verified. The conquistadors by all accounts have been both heroes and villains. Actually, the word is a fair and fancy name for a group of high-living, hot-blooded invaders, who took the land from the Indians. We're not going to repeat what's already been recorded. Our account starts with adventure, skips poetic intrigue and records mere happenstance.

The journals from which we take our early recorded history came from two separate houses in Saucelito. We can't vouch for the historical facts presented, but we've read the words that pioneers wrote, and writing them took dedication.

Finding Saucelito was accidental in a way, they both agreed; accidental but directly prompted by lust. There have been worse beginnings. The journals tell us that it was circa 1826 when a shipload of Atlantic coast malcontents loaded onto a barkentine vessel with instructions to the captain to 'Take us to the west coast and put us off when you reach that there sunny place we hear talk of.' That there sunny place was purported to be California.

The captain of the vessel was so cantankerous and onery he didn't deserve anything he ever got, short of the initial spark of life, which was none of his own doing. Those who knew him hoped he wouldn't die until he had paid back in misery the suffering he had caused in others. But they knew he couldn't, for no man could live that long and be that miserable. Ebekanezer Kane was his name. Vitality and lust his trademark. The fact that he got as far north as the Golden Gate was due to his lack of morals and his virile constitution. Two days out of Boston harbor he had bunked three female passengers in three separate parts of the vessel. After that he paid frequent calls on them throughout the voyage. The only fair thing he ever tried to do in his life was to make certain he vented his lickerous nature equally on the three women. The fact that he didn't have a head for figures made him spread his attention frequently; just in case. All the while this was going on the ship plowed on and on. He didn't notice the storm as the vessel rounded the Horn and headed north.

"Carry on," he continually told his first mate, who obeyed until they got to the Golden Gate where they were forced to stop for fresh water. The ship hove to in a small bay on her port side and several men went ashore to look for fresh water. Variety had always been the spice of life for Captain Kane, so when he spotted a young Indian lass on the beach, he ordered a boat and went ashore. She was a beautiful, plump maiden, with a round, fleshy face the color of a young chestnut in the sunshine. Any woman as pretty and engaging as she was had spent much time attracting suitors and nearly as much warding them off. She was wise in the latter business and knew immediately what bothered the captain. It didn't take a great mind for this because he was as obvious as a snake scrambling across a concrete slab, and nearly as fidgity. Her problem was getting the most out of him before he got anything out of her. It was a touch-and-go contest from the start. The captain thought he had run into an innocent beauty who would be proud of his attentions. He got nowhere with his hands while his mind was wandering from the effects of a native drink she was feeding him. After an hour of fumbling and frustration the captain excused himself and made off downhill where his men were getting water. "Tell the passengers I've found their home site," he said. "This is the paradise they were looking for, although it's a little hazy right now." He then ordered the ship to be unloaded on the double. He made his way back to the tent only to find that a young Indian brave had taken his place but was scoring better at the game, or the lass had lost defenses. Whichever it was the captain didn't like it. In fact it made him downright irritated. He decided to scare them up a little. Aiming his old blunderbuss with an unsteady hand and seeing double, he let fly at what he thought was an old stone urn. His aim was poor. The bullet struck the girl low on her anatomy and a little to one side; or to be exact, it ripped out a sizeable chunk of her buttock. It did little damage, except to her powers of attraction. From now on she'd

3

walk with an uneven ballast, thought the captain. The injury created far more commotion than it called for. In no time the tent was filled with neighbors all trying to stop the bleeding. This was no case for a medicine man. And the women trying to apply a tourniquet met with no success. The captain made his way back to the ship and found it empty of passengers. Enough crew members were present, and in a few minutes they had lifted anchor, hoisted sails and with a light ship managed to get away, with only a few broken arrows scratching the hull.

So a town was started. Who was responsible for its auspicious beginning? The captain: the lass? To give the town the benefit of a favorable legacy we think the Indian Maid's lack of permissiveness should get the credit.

2 T he site chosen for a new town was a far cry from 'that there sunny land' the easterners had in mind when they embarked on a new life. The area was aptly called Hurricane Gulch, and although the wind never reached hurricane velocity, it never gave up trying. Added to it was Pacific Ocean fog that blew down over the hill and covered the area with a constant damp coldness. But there was fresh water, deer, game, berries and Indians.

The Indians didn't stay long after the white settlers came to Saucelito. They were a peaceful tribe and accommodated to the persistent pushing and crowding of the white man. Little by little they filtered on up the gulch without standing their ground or balking in any way. This made some of the white invaders a little angry. They'd rather have a fight over the territory and get it settled. But no one would come to the war. The settlers did what they could; made laws and boundaries, and the colored people shrugged and acquiesced. Being more resourceful, the Indians could survive in new locations without much trouble. It didn't take long before all the Indians had moved out of their settlement and were ensconced on the hill tops above the

5

gulch. This left the whites to go about civilizing. But in less than a year the settlers realized the Indians had the best land for views of the entire San Francisco bay, while they, the whites, were engulfed in a foggy gulch. 'We're being taken advantage of,' they agreed, 'and besides, the best hunting grounds are up there. I tell you, we've got to get those people out of there once and for all.'

They were right, but for another reason: health. Their drinking water came from the creek and much of it was filtered through the Indian settlement above. Sanitation wasn't the Indian's strongest point. One white philosopher summed up the problem and gave the settlers a lasting and final cause for action. "Those Indians were stupid to allow us to stay in their midst in the first place. We don't want anyone that dumb to stay around us." A kind of mutual understanding came about. The Indians took a hint and gradually moved away.

Several years went by as the town grew into a sizeable settlement. By now boundaries were extended. Instead of staying in the fertile gulch entirely, adventurous newcomers were building houses on the steep hillside above the bay. It took a bit of doing, but once a structure was perched up there on poles and beams it was an aerie of some stability. Soon the whole hill had houses commanding one hundred eighty degree views of the bay and the Golden Gate.

During the historical period of gold, growth, amusement and activity in San Francisco, the little settlement across the bay slept on without absorbing any overflow. It was just as well, for all the men who came west seeking a fortune weren't exemplary people for any township. Most of the adventurers didn't know Saucelito existed, for it wasn't on maps and shouldn't have been.

In 1893, a portly self-appointed civic busybody started a campaign to incorporate Saucelito. There was no need for it. He thought they ought to have a police force of their own. Up 'til then a sheriff had patrolled the southern end of Marin

County whenever he thought of it. This unscheduled patrolling made crime risky. And anyway the residents of the town didn't need a policeman. They were content to raise peonies in their own backyard and had very little interest in what a neighbor was doing in his. The only squabbles of any consequence came about over property lines. Surveying, if any, had been done in a careless and casual way. The accuracy was questionable, and any man who had reclaimed a patch of land on a hillside, and carried rocks to bulkhead the real estate wanted to keep what his efforts had gained. Quarrels were always settled without major abrasions. But persistence paid off and the village got its incorporation papers in September of that year. Some said it only gave councilmen a license for graft. But they did get together and do one lasting thing; they agreed on the spelling of the name. Henceforth it would be Sausalito. The first historic meeting of the Sausalito City Council was held in a building located on the waterfront, where automobiles now park for the Ondine Restaurant.

The residents followed a peaceful routine most of the time. The men rode the ferry daily to San Francisco for work, returned, had a beer at the Arbordale, a historic old bar adjacent to the ferry slip, then hiked the steps leading to their cottages each evening. After doing some chores around the house they went to bed to rest for the next day's activities. Statistics show they rested well, for the population remained close to 2,000 from 1893 to 1906. This was the year nature took a look at San Francisco, found fault with its foundation, grabbed the spit of land by its scruff and shook the hell out of it, then tossed it aside like a discarded fish head. Everyone knows the result: fire, fear, destruction, desertion, waste, thievery, conniving, disease and death. Most of the people who fled the wrath moved back in. Many who escaped to Sausalito stayed in the little settlement. An abortive attempt to chase them out failed, as it should. Welcoming people one moment then pulling the rug out from under them the next doesn't leave you much moral ground to stand on. The point behind the ouster attempt was logical. The newcomers had to be smart to recognize the advantages of Sausalito living, or lazy do-nothings who couldn't face the monumental task of rebuilding the big city, or both. Either way the mayor didn't want them. He couldn't handle wise people and who needs lazy ones? But many stayed and were eventually absorbed. For years after that some of these people were quick to take credit for any good happening in the town, but refused to take any blame for the bad. A normal situation.

The completion of the Golden Gate bridge in 1939 was the start of destruction for Sausalito. After the bridge was built, land values in Sausalito skyrocketed. San Francisco was ten minutes away by automobile. The whole idea behind the project wasn't new. Each time a bridge was built over the Tiber in Roman times, land values near the bridge increased. The pattern remains.

The planning and vision of several men as to what a bridge would do to land values in Marin County was in its way as stupendous as constructing the bridge itself. The men mostly influential in the project were ambitious real estate investors. It's all too factual and boring to go into detail, but basically what they had to do was convince the voters of San Francisco that passing a bond issue for twelve million dollars to build the bridge would be in the people's economic interest. And this was during the height of the great depression. But it was done. And it was done by those land investors who, having read Henry George's 'Progress and Poverty' knew that there would be no changes in property tax laws. "George is right," they told themselves. Having digested his wisdom they decided to capitalize on the weakness in the system he warned about. Essentially, George proclaimed that the tax system meant progress for some and continued poverty for most. So the promoters bought up all the undeveloped land and many homes in and around Sausalito, then moved on up the county.

8

Soon they were property owners of great magnitude, and they put this weight to use. Their next investment was in a political campaign to pass the bond issue. They won and won and won. The railroads didn't believe the bond would pass, so didn't campaign against it. It has been reported that the men who influenced the Golden Gate Bridge realized a twenty million dollar profit from one and a half million dollar investment. A little extra frosting came from resale of the ferries, for somewhere along the line they had purchased the entire fleet.

A thick book of history could be written about the period between the completion of the Golden Gate Bridge and the demise of the ferries, but what happened was so predictable it isn't interesting. It happened quickly. The trains from Marin County continued to bring commuters to Sausalito where they rode the ferry to San Francisco, but the attrition had started, progress in another direction was being encouraged. Bus service expanded, automobiles were purchased, and soon the entire old system of commuting by train and ferry dribbled away. It was sad to see a system that did a job so well die out for another no better, just different. In less than a year after the bridge was built the ferries were gone, the trains derailed, the tracks rusted, the old Arbordale restaurant out of the business of tranquilizing for profit. Private automobiles were in.

3 City Hall was functioning by habit and routine, taking care of problems it could handle and ignoring innovative suggestions. It was seldom that any of the latter were presented, but when planning was mentioned it got the attention one expected: 'that's future and who can predict the future?' An agenda in 1938 carried items such as: what to do about the acacia trees leaning precariously toward Spencer Street in the 900 block? We should have a pole erected for a new fire siren; we got the whistle in the last budget, but no place to put it. El Monte Lane should be roughened up so people won't slip and fall. The roots of those gum trees on Bulkley Ave. have blocked the main sewer line again. There were other items, but these were the most important. The budget to operate the town was a staggering $62,000 annually. There were 15 employees; a city hall clerk, a few policemen and firemen and a small street crew.

Sausalito couldn't escape attracting unusual people, some famous, some infamous, some popular, but most notorious. They came and went at their own convenience and safety. Who knows the number of outlaws that holed up in the old Valhalla down in Hurricane Gulch while waiting for the pressure of pursuit to pass? That building still stands. It's a restaurant now, but it was originally built to house tired seamen who wanted to get their land legs back while waiting for another ship. A boarding house with a strange name. Literally it means 'Hall of the slain.' The more popular meaning is 'Norwegian heaven for sea faring men.' It was built in 1838 at the mouth of the fresh water creek where Captain Kane landed. In the early days there was good business in selling fresh water to ships that anchored in the harbor. The water was piped into the Valhalla on one side and out the other where the shore boats could conveniently tie up and fill their flagons and barrels. In the meantime the seamen drank a strong concoction so bad it would cure alcoholism in a normal person. When two or three shiploads of seamen gathered in the bar waiting for the barrels to fill, the proprietor cut down the supply of fresh water to a trickle. It was one of the earliest methods known to control commerce. Later a new proprietor had women available who occupied rooms upstairs. When that innovation was installed, the water supply looked as if it were drying up.

There wasn't much change in operation of the Valhalla until prohibition days. During those years it was rum runners' headquarters. Everybody knew it, including the feds. Whenever they raided the place they carried off gallons of evidence, but the liquid decoy was a swill so bad it would rot the hold of a ship. After prohibition the building lay empty for decades, deteriorating slowly for it was made of good materials. Then life came again during World War II when workers at the Sausalito shipyard filled the rooms at hot-sheet rates. It wasn't until 1948 that an enterprising woman bought the structure and turned the lower floor into a restaurant. The upstairs was left for idle gossip.

When Jack London came to live in Sausalito for a short time, he passed up the Valhalla and roomed in a house one hundred yards further along the waterfront. The house still stands on the curve at Richardson and Bridgeway. A million automobiles pass within five feet of the house each year. *Sea Wolf*, one of London's greatest novels, was published in 1904. The beginning of the book describes a Sausalito-to-San Francisco ferry encounter with a ship in mid-stream in the dark of night. A few men who thought they were being rescued were shanghaied and woke up as crewmen on the *Sea Wolf*, far at sea. The idea for the beginning of the book came to London while he was living in Sausalito. From his room he had a direct view of the ferry runs. Jack London didn't stay long in Sausalito. He didn't stay long anywhere. He couldn't and be in all the places he was during the short time he lived. But the house is referred to as the Jack London house.

Moving further north along the waterfront, only another two hundred yards or so, one sees a huge stone structure with several round turret-like buttresses. Atop this stone wall is a house. The story of why the wall stood for forty years before a house was built on it is worth noting.

In 1910 a man who owned an empire decided to build a house in Sausalito. W. R. Hearst was his name. He told his underlings what he wanted and the wheels were set in motion. The hillside was purchased, plans were made and presented to the lord, changed a few times, and finally approved. This was to be no ordinary house. It was going to be San Simeon. Work began. The most impressive stone fortress-like foundation ever built on the west coast was erected. It had to be immense to hold up the hillside from falling into the bay, and to support the edifice the architects had planned. The wall was 600 feet long and 90 feet high. At the base it was 20 feet thick. The wall was 300 feet from the water's edge and 100 feet above it. The massive half round buttresses added further support, design and beauty. It was an impressive monument to hard labor. But that's as far as it got. The town councilmen awoke one day to discover the huge stone scar on the hillside and started asking questions. The building inspector was a part time employee, and worked very little of that.

"Yes, there was some talk about building a house on top of the stone wall," he told the council. "Some men came to see me and the plans they had were pretty elaborate I'll have to admit. They were talking about a walkway a hundred feet high from the house out to the water, with an elevator down to a boat dock."

Further questioning revealed that a building permit had not been issued. "The men told me there were some details to work out with Mr. Hearst and then they'd be back. I guess they forgot." He dropped Mr. Hearst's name as casually as he ran the building inspection department.

It was the first time the councilmen had heard that the man planned to be a resident of their community. A couple of them were impressed to think that they had chosen a place to live that also appealed to the big man. "Not many people are ahead of Hearst," one remarked. That wasn't enough to impress the majority and they issued a stop work order on the project. They'd have to look into the situation. Ignoring the authority of small town authoritarians is a mistake.

In the meantime townpeople heard of the affront, learned a little about the plans, and for whom the building was planned. For the first time in history a majority of the citizens agreed with the council. Strange alliances were formed. Even the fighting factions of the Episcopalians and

Presbyterians came to an agreement. Rumors throughout the town grew fast and absurd. One such was that Clarence Darrow was going to argue the case for Hearst. He'd put those small town politicians in their place. This was the most absurd rumor, for Hearst would rather give up a printing press than to have such a social-minded man as Darrow speak for him. Nothing came of the build-up for a showdown. Hearst got interested in more earth shaking projects and completely forgot about Sausalito. It was a let-down for the citizens, like preparing for a duel and having your opponent sneak out at the last moment.

Honest reasons seldom become history, and it happened again in this instance. Here was a simple case of no building permit, stop work, delays, then changed plans and other interests. But Sausalito picked up a rumor for the reason the project was stopped, and because it gave the town a little distinction, although false, the community has traded on it ever since.

The story started when a group of residents were discussing the wall, the plans and Hearst in the Old Arbordale Saloon, and while beer and other spirits lubricated their minds and imaginations, it also produced skepticisms. One man was Tony Guidi, the stone mason who was foreman on the job.

"You've got it all wrong," he told the group, "sure the architect didn't get a permit, but that could have been taken care of in a couple days. Everybody knows that. You think Sausalito could stop Hearst? No sir. What happened is that a couple of those town trustees got on their high horse to show their blue noses. You see, a lot of people don't like Hearst because of the way he started up his newspaper business writing all that sensational stuff, and using pictures the way he does. It gets people wrought up, you know. There's no telling where he'll end. Then, too, there's that Spanish American war that some people say he started by writing so much about Cuba. Anyway, I tell you those trustees said they didn't want

14

a man like Hearst living in Sausalito and they were going to prevent it. They got a lot of people behind them who said they'd back 'em up. I guess it's easy to find people who think they're better than someone else."

Tony's words had just enough plausibility to make them believable, and enough fascination to make them interesting. So the story went around that the council stopped the project because most residents didn't want Hearst living in Sausalito. Such is history.

The wall stood until 1948, when Dr. Wiper purchased the property and built a house on it. It's a showplace home with access from the street above. A hillevator takes occupants from the parking area, down a steep incline 150 feet to the house below.

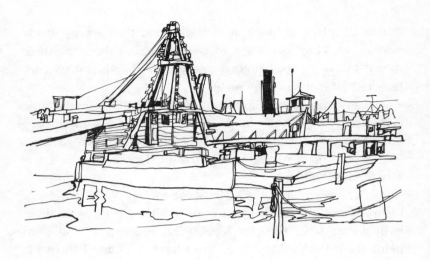

4   The geography of Sausalito is nearly all uphill. This is great for views but has been the cause of numerous squabbles over the years. No one was particular about surveys in the pioneer days and even if one wanted to survey, it was difficult to lay out lots and boundaries on a forty-degree slope. There was enough land for the few odd people who wanted to live on a steep hillside in an undeveloped town, and no one ever believed the area was going to amount to much. Surveying for the fussy was done with a plumb bob and a yardstick; the casual never went to that trouble. The big disagreements came many years later when zoning and other sophisticated laws were written. The wording in those ordinances had to have a grandfather clause every other paragraph which made what they called 'legal non-conforming uses' out of almost all properties. Actually the phrase is a euphemism to cover up the favoritism that occurred in the days when cliques and claques, cronies and caprice ruled the town. In this way Sausalito isn't much different from most small towns. But there had to be a lot of lenience on some people's part when easements were necessary to make public paths so citizens could get to their property. They make nice walks now, and visitors think the town was cleverly laid out. Old timers remember when the paths were petunia patches and begonia beds.

What brought the artists, writers and other creative people to Sausalito in the 1930s and 1940s was a combination of the physical layout of the town, the charm and quaintness, the slow pace, the uncommercialization, the low cost of living and the unparalleled views. Artists understand and recognize beauty quicker than laymen, so it was not surprising they chose Sausalito. They came, looked around, and many started building flimsy shelter on the cheapest land they could find: free. This was the waterfront a little north of the business district. Mostly the shelter was floating to start with, but when the craft leaked relentlessly and got to be too much trouble to keep afloat, something had to be done. One ingenious man worked out a solution. He drove numerous pilings in the mud surrounding his houseboat, and when the highest tide of the year came floating the house high, he worked beams under the floor, then secured them to the pilings. When the tide receded he was left high and dry. Others followed the method and soon an entire colony was established, perched on spindly pilings with long rickety ramps leading to them. Many of the houses still stand. An occasional high tide combined with waves laps water at the floors, reminding the occupants of their beginnings.

The land where the artists moved in, built and pirated, was not public land free to the taking. It was privately owned and undeveloped because no one in their right mind would live on it. When the tide came in it was four feet of water, but with no water the area was a stinking mess of rotting

17

water-soaked logs, decaying organic wastes, silt and mud, dead fish and trapped marine life. It may have been ecologically sound, but the gasses were questionable. The houseboats were fragile and sparse, and no one, let alone the owner of the land if he knew, believed they would survive a winter's storm. Later when the colony proved it was there to stay, some of the landlords asked for and got a few dollars rent from some of the occupants. From others they got promises.

How underwater land got to be privately owned in the first place is another example of Sausalito's uniqueness.

It started back in 1860, or thereabouts, when General Vallejo was passing through Sausalito on his way to Sonoma. A celebration was going on in the settlement that turned out to be half potlatch and half plain old frontier hell raising. The general was an active man; physical games roused his spirits. He quickly got into the swing of the festival and at the close of a hard fought battle between two remaining contestants trying to get to the top of a huge rock, and inflicting enough contusions on each other to satisfy a medical school, he announced the next contest. He would give all the land to the winner of a rock throwing contest that fell within the boundaries of two stones thrown at right angles to each other. The only hitch was that the land couldn't contain property that had a house on it. That didn't leave much real estate, but it brought out some formidable contestants. They tossed enough stones uphill, down and across, to make the area look like a battlefield of falling shrapnel. Muscular Cy Waldo, part Indian, mostly arms, was sitting in the Valhalla saloon limbering up his elbow by frequent bending. This took considerable exercise, for he had arms that reached well below his knees and were as supple on a good day as boiled spaghetti. He hadn't considered entering the contest, for he didn't want to own land. It stared at you, coldly inviting work, and he didn't see how he could work any more than he did. But he wouldn't mind owning some territory if it didn't worry him.

18

Suddenly a thought came to him. He'd toss a pebble across that channel down there, and half way to the other side of the bay, then he could charge people for fishing over his land. The main appeal was that water doesn't demand work. It can't go bad on you if you don't do anything to it. Cy couldn't ever remember hearing of water erosion. And besides it's pretty to look at; beautiful if you own it. Conditions were ideal. The tide was out, there was land, with no houses on it. After all contestants had finished Cy showed up. He braced himself on the bank, wound up his long arm, and when it recoiled the rock shot out over the mud for close to 500 feet. Then he duplicated that feat at right angles, and in less than three minutes he had acquired 250,000 square feet of real estate.

The general stood good on his promise and accorded a deed of ownership for the underwater property to long armed Cy Waldo. The deed has changed hands many times, but the land has remained privately owned, and has caused enough legal disputes to start a whole new court of justice.

5   Like all small towns Sausalito had a group of people who thought they could run the town better than anyone else, so they did. A combination of civic pride and confidence was about all that was necessary in the early days to be on the political inside. Talent was never considered, but some gained it through experience. What the councilmen did and what they didn't do shaped the town. But to blame them for not thinking of the future and

20

thereby making ordinances for guidance would be asking too much of a man. On the other hand, if you're going to blame them for lack of foresight, you must also credit them for things they did do. It evens out.

The best show in town in the '40s was the monthly council meeting. This was mainly due to the cast of characters, but the physical aspects of the building contributed to the show too.

The city hall wasn't much to start with and had been going downhill ever since. The building had thick brick walls on each side for a little fire protection from flimsily built business houses adjoining it, and a thick wall in back which also served as a bulkhead to prevent the hillside from sliding down and crashing into the offices. The front of the building was glass with a view of the bay. The second floor housed the library, which wasn't used very much. The stairs were long and rickety, which discouraged old people, and the books were not interesting enough to encourage the young.

The city hall meeting room could seat about one hundred people, but the informed ones didn't sit down. The seats were old fold down wooden affairs, misaligned, broken, slanty and risky. This encouraged standing, making it easier to slip out for a sustaining shot of whiskey next door. The most significant aspect of the meeting room was the jail, located in a small back room up against the bulkhead wall, with the entrance at one side of the raised platform where the councilmen sat. Occasionally during a meeting, a policeman would wrestle an alleged violator up the aisle and put him in jail. Fortunately his protests were not recorded by the person taking the minutes, even though they were spoken at a public meeting.

One night when Luke Bradford got happily drunk celebrating his wife's leaving him for Isaac the fisherman, he was led up the aisle toward the jail door. He saw the array of sober city officials seated on the raised dais and shouted,

"It's a frame-up. You've already got the judge and jury waiting for me."

Sausalito was lucky to have a city hall staff of proud and dedicated women who knew more about the town and what was going on than the mayor. There were only two workers, and sometimes three when work piled up. All of them were capable, honest, straightforward and devoted people who thought of their duties in much the same way as a watchman patrolling a large plant feels responsible for the company's stock. Any one of them could account for every penny of the city's treasury at any given moment. There wasn't much, but that didn't reduce their zealous sense of duty. Sausalito was their town and they did everything they could to make it look good.

Most towns operate on their property taxes and Sausalito was no exception. The methods used to appraise houses often appeared peculiar. One could imagine that if city hall needed a new wheelbarrow, a dollar was added to the taxes of ten or twelve houses to buy one. If something more costly and sophisticated was needed, those houses in the higher bracket could better afford it, and might get assessed accordingly. No one complained. Other monies to operate the town came from the state, based on population. A running census was kept corresponding with building permits. The remainder of the budget money came from sales taxes, business license, dog license, which amounted to more than business license, cigarette tax, traffic fines (minuscule), building permits, subventions and, surprisingly, several hundred dollars from library fines. Seems it was too much trouble to climb the stairs and return books in time.

A typical meeting in the '40s will help to show how the town got shaped the way it did. It makes one wonder how any town could survive. But if the truth were known, Sausalito government was not unlike that of any other town in the U.S. Most of the business was trivial, but the councilmen

22

were good and fair and acted as if the continued spinning of the earth depended upon every decision they made. As they sat in their cushioned seats shuffling reams of papers, a few dozen or so citizens were boisterously greeting and back slapping one another waiting for the show to start. At last the gavel of authority. After the roll call the minutes were read and usually approved without a change. Then the agenda for the night's meeting was read aloud. Everything democratic.

"One: Mrs. Prosser wants permission to cut down some acacia trees in front of her property on Central Ave. that are on the street right of way. The roots get into her sewer line and plug it up."

"Let her cut her own trees," someone shouted from the audience.

"Two: Something happened to the fire alarm box on the corner of Locust and Caledonia streets and it burned out."

"Get a new one."

"Three: Two people have requested lights on the corner of Third and North streets. Another party wants one between Richardson and Main."

"Whoever heard of a street light in the middle of the block?"

The citizens solved problems quickly, but the councilmen would have to discuss pros and cons.

"Four: The police chief says we need a new flag pole in the park. Termites got to it.

"Five: The fire chief requests a new pole for the main fire whistle."

"Two poles in one meeting?"

The man who offered most of the quick problem solutions was ordinarily a talkative old timer, but he hadn't learned when to keep his mouth shut. He had run for a city council seat a time or two but been defeated because he couldn't stop talking. He was both a contradiction and a hard learner.

23

"Six: There's that 'No U turn' business on Bridgeway that wasn't decided on at the last meeting."

There were other items of equal importance, then the committee reports, and if there was time a discussion on a zoning ordinance. Certainly not priority.

When finished the mayor exhibited more mannerisms than a pantomimist, rubbed his chin, shifted in his seat, hunched his shoulders, coughed and proclaimed:

"Yes, yes. Now let's see. Yes. Good. All right. Now where were we?" He seemed surprised that he was present at a public meeting. After a little struggle with his thoughts he introduced the first item of business, but that only lasted until Bill Pascam, an inveterate complainer, realized that the agenda was finished and the public was allowed to speak.

"Your Honor," he said, "I'd like to address the council on a very important matter." His words came clear and distinct from around a fresh cigar.

The mayor looked up. "Ah, er, yes, well, ah Bill, can you wait until . . ."

"No, I can't wait. This is important. You councilmen up there don't know what's going on in this town. I spend all my time here, not just sleep here like you fellows who spend all day in San Francisco. I know what's going on. Now what I want to say is that you've got no consideration for the older people in this town. I tell you, you don't realize how hard it is for people on pensions to get along. Maybe your wages increase all the time but pensions don't. I'd like to see you try to live on a pension. You couldn't do it. Why I can walk down the street any day and talk to a dozen or more citizens on pensions, and they say to me, 'Bill, you're the only one in this town who realizes how hard it is for us to get along.' Well, let me tell you I do know. And what's more, I care. That's more than you can say. Sitting up there week after week, spending money, increasing taxes. So I want to know what you're going to do about it. There's got to be an end to

24

it." As he warmed up to his usual subject, he chewed harder on the cigar. This was the signal the audience and the council-men looked for. As he chewed and mouthed the cigar he created more saliva, and not wanting to swallow the fluid, or being in a position to spit it out, he could only talk and chew until his mouth was filled. He continued with his boring speech, spouting accusations without basis, groping and feel-ing his way along, hoping he'd hit upon some idea he could enlarge upon. Logic never came to his mind, but that didn't stop him from talking. As the level of the liquid in his mouth grew he was forced to tip his head back to prevent it running out. In a short time he was gargling every word. The end was in sight. But not until he was talking to the ceiling, and sound-ing like a man going down for the third time did he stop. Bill was a hard loser. As he made his way blindly toward the aisle he couldn't look down, but he continued mumbling under murky water. When he got to the aisle someone turned him in the right direction, opened the door and he walked out to flood the gutter. Bill would go home after that.

This performance had been going on for several years. If an aisle sitter had ever turned Bill in the opposite direction it just might have put an end to council meetings.

The meeting was about average. It had been learned a long time before that it was better to let citizens speak when they wished than be accused of being undemocratic. Before adjournment two inmates were put in jail, the city attorney had nearly two hours of uninterrupted sleep, and there were reams of notes for the next meeting's minutes when it would be learned if the fire chief got a new pole for the siren.

6   Sausalito contributed heavily to the war effort.
It is still paying for the contribution. In 1942
a shipyard was built on the north end of town that
employed 27,000 workers; that was quite a load
for a small town to carry. But the good residents
swallowed their pride and turned patriotic. Nearly
every house rented rooms, built more rooms, apartments, sleeping quarters, sheds and cabins, and
some went so far as to leave their automobiles outside in all kinds of weather to make sleeping quarters out of their garages. It was gratifying to see the
sacrifice made to help the country win the war.
City Hall, of course, encouraged the conversions
and never asked for building permits. It couldn't
have kept up with the applications if it had. Many
illegalities were overlooked during the war; housing

was but one. But encouraging citizens to accommodate factory workers one year and expecting them to tear out partitions the next is asking too much of profits and patriotism.

During the height of employment in the shipyard most citizens expected that sales taxes on commodities sold in bars and restaurants would swell the coffers of the city treasury. This expectation was from those not close to the local government. They only thought of it because they paid their property taxes, and taxes are about all that most people know about government. But city hall didn't think about the sales tax possibility. It had other and more important things on its mind. And the councilmen were too busy conducting the city business that came before them to be dreaming up new problems to work on. So with a payroll of fifteen million dollars a month being paid in Sausalito for nearly four years, the town got nothing out of it for the treasury. The shipyard compiled a record of 172 ships launched and was responsible for a multitude of illegal apartments.

In a round-about way the shipyard contributed more to the development of Sausalito after it was abandoned than it did during the height of its activity. After the war, government security was strict in guarding the 60 acres and numerous buildings, but as the war memories faded, so did appropriations for security. The huge 'KEEP OUT, GOVERNMENT PROPERTY' signs bleached and faded and appeared less authoritative. Soon there were no guards around. After that the attrition set in fast with the help of eager and ambitious young men. Most of them were from the waterfront, needing material to build a houseboat. In a few years the buildings were moved piece by piece a few hundred yards to the north where material was rearranged into living quarters for houseboat dwellers.

The old abandoned shipyard steadily became an ecological eyesore. Sixty acres of rotted, deteriorated buildings, huge rusty piles of metal, acres of asphalt once smooth and heavily

27

trafficked, now cracked and humping and breaking up by green weeds and fennel. Only since 1970 has there been a little development in the area. The reason it hadn't been built on is that the city could never decide on the best zoning for the area. This was a case where no plan was the best plan. Adjacent to the shipyard is the Gate 5 area.

At one time there was a gate to let workers into the shipyard, but it's long since gone and now the area is as wide open as the Golden Gate and as inviting as a revival meeting. This is where the houseboat colony is located. Geographically it is not within the city limits of Sausalito, but its influence reaches far beyond imaginary lines, and is largely responsible for shaping the town's character and reputation. Gate 5 is where many artists live. The creative processes that go on in that group of people would challenge the first six days of the universe. But before one gets to the houseboats, there are fringes to pass.

On the corner of Bridgeway and Gate 5 road is a service station. The people living directly behind it are the big users of the station's free facilities. These people live in trucks, autos, trailers, station wagons, boarded up garages, tents, lean-tos and in good weather simply in a sleeping bag. The trucks display the most varied construction; God-awful gothic would be a kind definition. These portable poachers on public street, railroad right of way and private property, who move on when pressure and/or whim motivates them, have built structures with facets and angles that would strain a bevel square. Guided for the most part by utilitarian needs, secondly by what free materials are available, they let their creative imagination go wild. Chimneys protrude from the back, sides or top, whichever is easiest to cut a hole in, cupboards, shelves and windows make angles that defy balance and engineering. And then the whole mess is painted with whatever paint can be found. Color? Who cares? These structures are homes, parked in the summer dust or winter mud

28

among debris ranging from anchors to broken zithers. The people are young and hardy nomads from a normal and easier way of life, Berkeley braceros, vagabonds and vagrants, all wandering, seeking, and wondering what they are seeking. But they harm no one. The private land they park on is not used for anything, and people have to live somewhere. Sociability and cooperation among the group is superb. A person on foot entering the area would have no trouble getting a meal and a place to sleep. But this stranger would take his chances on getting more than he asked for. The group unwittingly gave away as much hepatitis as hospitality. Frequently the police would invade the area when pot got too pervasive, to roust, harass, and arrest, but the effort was futile, for it did little good to protect society at large. Pushers of drugs never lived in such low style. It was a normal situation; the victims were the target.

Beyond this little colony toward the water, the large houseboats are tied up. This is not a neat marina in a rich San Francisco suburb. There are no safe and sturdy docks, strong cleats, a safe flotation, bright colored nylon ropes, flags or order. Gate 5 is as much a catastrophe as a convenience. But these shoreside houseboats have utilities. Electric wires of all sizes run from the company-provided poles. There's no pattern, no order. The wires are so thick they look like a field of Maypoles in a huge tangle. A bat would have a hell of a time flying through them. When high tide comes in, the wires hang dangerously close to the gangplanks, thereby narrowing the gap to electrocution. At low tide, the wires are nearly taut. No one knows who pays for whose electricity. The wires are sneaked in and pirated, some by-pass meters altogether, which keeps the utility company busy checking the area. The company men have snipped more illegal electric wires in Gate 5 than wholesale rustlers have snipped barbed wire in Texas. The water supply is much the same. Long hoses and pipes lead from the main, then branch off to feed a house, another

29

house, robbing force and leaving only a trickle of irritation. Fortunately there are no toilets to fill and flush.

There are two large ferries at Gate 5. Two unusual people live in them. Varda has one and Jon Dane another. Jon lives in the old Clementina. She's rotting away at a fast clip, but there's a lot left, too. Like an iceberg, a good part of her is sunk in the mud, which gives her a stubborn, solid appearance. Jon's tenancy of the Clementina came about in an unusual manner. But that's not surprising; unusual things often happen to Jon. The owner of the land is a rich man, a little on the eccentric side but large on shrewdness. He bought the ferry for salvage, moved her onto his property, then didn't have the heart to tear her apart. Jon pays no rent; he's the caretaker. He suggested to the owner that he live there to keep an eye on the vessel.

"Go ahead," said Don Arques, the owner, "but you'll have to move when the city lets me tie up to the sewer main, because I'll be developing the property down there."

"Of course," replied Jon.

It's been a French provisional arrangement since 1951; good for fourteen years, renewable without question once, the second time after a little discussion. The ferry is still there, the land undeveloped because the city won't allow Arques to connect to the main until he either tears down all the shacks and houseboats or makes them conform to the building code. He argues that they can't conform unless they are connected to the sewer line. While the confrontation continues, more houseboats are built. This pleases Arques because it displeases the city.

Jon moved onto the huge vessel and after fixing up a room for himself, he let others come aboard and do the same. After all, he's the caretaker and he's keeping an eye on her as he agreed. There's a whole colony living on the ferry. In every conceivable corner a wall or two has been built to provide a little privacy, so that one can stake out a claim and set up
30

housekeeping. In some places, the walls consist of only a cloth curtain. No one expects complete privacy; everybody knows what goes on behind walls; it doesn't matter what the walls consist of. The main deck is as wide open as a prairie and no more inviting than an open grave. Yet a dozen or more young people live there in the summertime. When winter winds whistle through, the population thins out. Where they go is not entirely known. Some double up with others in more protected rooms, a few share houseboats, other absorption is practiced; a sort of community commensalism takes place.

Because the ferry is so large and high, she commands more open space around her than any houseboat. Sticking out of the sides are tubes and pipes which discharge indiscriminate wastes at unscheduled times. Coupled with the force of gravity the pipes are authoritative. This is sanitation; at least for the room from which it emanates. It's a sad day when a newcomer brings his boat in looking for a place to tie up, gets too close to the ferry, and someone aboard satisfies an urge. One of the favorite pastimes is to watch a boat come in. Children gather at windows to observe. 'Hey dad, come and watch. Boy, they're gonna get it.' When it happens, the air turns blue with curses.

During extreme low tide, Gate 5 is no place to visit. Not until the great Pacific Ocean moves back in and the flushing action takes place is it acceptable. It can get pretty bad while waiting. As one resident said: "Our effluent is affluent."

There's still another group living at Gate 5. They live in floating objects anchored out in the bay a few hundred yards. They have no fresh water, no sanitary facilities, no heat, no artery to society, and very little comfort. Each time they row to shore, they carry a gallon bottle or so to fill with fresh water from the service station. Cooking, if any, is done on small propane stoves. If the quality is good enough to keep out dampness, their sleeping bags are the only comfort. The

31

walls of the vessels drip with condensation which feeds the ever-growing mold. Eating habits are varied, of course, but the Gate 5 flotilla is where you'll find a heavy concentration of macrobiotic diet followers, grains and raw foods, more for convenience than dedication. The whole of Gate 5 is so crowded it would make Hong Kong harbor look like a model of strict zoning.

Four or five hundred people live in the area. Many are bright, creative and interesting, and many are bores. Not much different in that respect from any neighborhood. What they have in common is the wish to escape paying rent. Most of them put up with more disagreeableness than a human deserves to accomplish this aim. And they have to be careful about introducing comfort for fear it may be conventional on the outside. To gain their freedom they have rules and customs which are often more strict than those they are trying to escape from.

The waterfront dwellers have been criticized for everything from atheism to Zen Buddhism. They'll admit to most, but the one charge they steadfastly deny is that they are wholesale polluters of the environment. It's true they don't have weekly garbage pickup, but they don't need it. "We have very few excesses," they claim, "none of us could fill a garbage can in six months. We don't buy canned foods because we don't have that kind of money, and it's a poor bargain anyway. Nor T.V. dinners with their aluminum throw away plates, or packaged foods that have wrappers and containers to dispose of. Most of us make our own beer, so there's no cans. Just think of the numbers of indestructible soap, bleach and polish containers the people on the hill toss into garbage cans weekly. Why, they're filling the land with garbage. Every time there's a semi-annual cleanup in town you'll see enough junk tossed out to fill a large crater. Take those aluminum deck chairs and chaise longues for example. You see enough of them discarded each time to provide the Queen Mary, and

32

all that's wrong with them is the plastic webbing needs replacing, but it's too much trouble, they'll buy new ones next summer. The manufacturers have a hard time maintaining a supply, but those consumers are doing their best to sustain the shortage."

When it comes to the raw sewage charge, the waterfront people cite the huge Pacific Ocean with its voluminous tide action twice a day. Then they quickly point out that their sewage provides much needed bacteria to the bay waters to keep the environment alive, which otherwise would quickly starve from the sterile sewage that comes out of the treatment plant. A balance is needed and houseboat dwellers help provide it.

One complaint often heard about Gate 5 people was that they were so dirty. 'It's downright indecent,' some said.

It's true very few of the houseboats had facilities for bathing, and the people knew better than to dip into the bay waters. But everyone likes a little comfort, so a few of the men got together and built a community shower on the edge of the shore, near the gangplank leading to the ferry San Rafael.

The shower was strictly a utilitarian affair. What else? A large piece of plywood was laid on the ground. On one end stood a water heater connected to gas and water. The other end was the shower pan. A slight slope toward the bay served as drainage. Another piece of plywood stood vertical against the water tank to shield it from splashing water. A bent piece of pipe extended in a long arm from the top of the heater, ending in a shower head. Valves stuck through the plywood for mixing hot and cold water. First class! That's all. The other three sides were open. Did it meet the building code? Whose? It was vented to the sky where all vents ultimately end. The drain water went to the ocean.

Who paid for the gas and water? Don Arques, who else? Did he give permission? He wasn't asked. They knew better than to bother Arques with such trivia.

The shower area became a gathering place. A little like an old stove in an old community store. As someone showered conversation continued. Modesty? Men and women alike were plainly saying, "I don't care what you see, but you know I'm clean." The shower was a huge success.

City and county officials and busybody citizens continued to complain of indecency. It's difficult to satisfy everyone. The earlier complaints said that the people were indecent and dirty, now they said the people were indecent but clean. Improvement.

7 on Dane came to Sausalito in a round-about
way, taking more side trips than most inhabitants. He's a slender man of questionable age, with
a quick and youthful mind. He has a kind face that
looks a bit elfish, with small eyes set deep behind
thick eyebrows. Jon is an insatiable reader and an
incisive inquisitor. He was born in New York City,
attended public schools for a short time, then his
formal education ended abruptly in the sixth grade.
After that, he claimed, his real education started
and he never attended another class. What happened
in the sixth grade to cause the momentous decision
had been growing for a long time, but on that particular day he carefully listened to the teacher for a

change, and realized it had always been the same; the teacher was on an ego trip.

"All teachers were," he said, "they so thoroughly explained every problem and answered every question that there was nothing left to think about. They discouraged thinking and who can remember anything if they don't think about it? So I wasn't learning the why of anything, the theory, the maxim. It was a disgrace." So he announced to his father he was quitting school and the reason why. His father didn't interfere except to say he would check on his son from time to time to see if he was reading and learning. Jon read constantly, and learned. But it took one more shake-up for him to realize that books are one world, people are another.

At the age of seventeen he went out to get a job. "All right," the man said, "You show up at seven each morning and go home at four. A half hour for lunch. Start Monday." Before Monday came he had given the idea much thought. He went to his father.

"I got the job," he said, "but I don't think it's right that someone should buy my life, my time."

"But you told the man it was for sale."

"Yes," said Jon, "but that doesn't make it right, and you've always said I should do the right thing."

During a long discussion the father explained that a job represents income, money is security against wants and needs, security is a feeling that seems to agree with human nature.

"But that leaves no challenge," argued Jon. "Without challenge there's no inducement, so why live? I will not sell my life to that man or any man. I hereby declare that each morning when I awaken I will not have money or security, as you call it, to carry me through the day. In that way each day will be a challenge to me."

For a seventeen-year-old, a declaration such as that was a momentous one. But Jon has stayed with his declaration. He never has excess money, but he is never wanting.

When he came to California from Chicago he was fresh off a stint in the Communist Party. California was a new challenge, one that appealed to his nature. That nature seemed to lead him into choosing means of making a living about as unprofitable as writing poetry. He took up talc mining in the Panamint Mountains. He found the soapstone all right, but getting it out proved to be as slippery as the product itself. He hadn't given that aspect of the operation much thought. He quit mining after he met Eva. She was the first woman he had ever met that pleased, satisfied and excited him. They lived together in Lone Pine while he did odd jobs and she concentrated on the subliminal. She was oddly occult, and said she was "with him" while he was away spreading manure or digging post holes. Jon didn't always feel her presence, but she was always home when he returned, and that was enough for him. One day he returned unexpectedly to find her concentrating and consorting with his employer in such a way it looked impossible to "be with him."

"But why, Eva? Why?" he asked her.

"Oh, Jon," she said, "I'm sorry. Really I am. Jon, on the physical plane you have no peer. You are superb. And on the mental plane your stimulation is of the highest calibre, and not wanting. But Jon, oh Jon, on the astral plane I must reject you."

"That's alright," said Jon, packing his few belongings. "I'm more disappointed in Al for hiring me under false pretenses."

For a man of Jon's philosophy and ability Sausalito is an ideal place to live. He became a gardener, and besides doing a little work in gardens he cultivates plants on the decks of the ferry, experiments on soils and conditioners, reads, thinks, is useful to people and enjoys life. He is an independent man. On the practical side he can repair all plumbing problems, he understands electricity, his automobile is no mystery to him and he's an expert carpenter. But he never hires himself out for any job except gardening, and only enough of that to satisfy a few needs. Most of his time is spent in fighting the forces of the bay to keep his ferry afloat.

One day Jon was working in Mrs. Summers' garden. She hired him as much for his conversation as his work. He could do both and she could afford it.

"No, I don't agree with you," he said, deftly pruning a rose bush. "Most people on the waterfront are extremely moral and commit few sins."

"Do you mean to say those beatniks, or Bohemians or whatever they're called, go by any rules at all?" asked Mrs. Summers. "Why I never. Just look at their clothes, and their long hair. Everybody knows they're lazy, dirty, immoral and a disgrace to the community. Artistic, humph!" She pursed her lips as tight as a new zipper.

"Ha!" laughed Jon. "You depend upon them. Almost all the clothes they wear come from the Salvage Shop you women operate. They keep you in business. And lazy? Why, that's not true. They work enough to provide their needs. Because their needs don't include inessentials, they don't have to work eight hours a day every day. Their work is bread labor. You see, they buy leisure with their philosophy, time to do what they want to do. Your society buys ulcers, and little slips of paper that tell of payments you made on things you don't need. You pay heavily for the intangibles you never think about." He paused. When she didn't speak he continued. "Really, I don't know about morals. I'm not sure what it means. Do you know?"

"Well, just take the fact that most of them that live together aren't married. That's enough right there."

"Oh, really? Ha! There's no divorce, no scandals, no costs to taxpayers for courts and jails. You ought to be pleased. Somebody has to pay for courts, jails, police, lawyers to handle those messes your society creates. And remember, when there's no marriage, there can be no premarital inter-

38

course, which you frown upon, nor can a husband be cuck-
olded. That's worth something, isn't it? Can you hill people
say the same?" He felt so good about his logic he accidentally
clipped the main stem of an eight foot clematis vine.

Mrs. Summers was furious, both because of the vine,
and because she'd lost an argument.

"Look what you've done," she cried. "Oh, how could
you be so foolish? I should have known better than to allow
anyone like you on my property. You people have no respect
for anything. I've known it all the time. You can't be trusted.
I should have listened to Alice." For anyone having so many
facts and then acting against them she had a right to be angry.

Jon tried to express his regrets, but she interrupted.

"I don't believe it for one minute. I think you did it on
purpose. You people hate us. You're all the time poking fun at
us and trying to make us look old fashioned and foolish.
Sorry. Huh!"

"Mrs. Summers," said Jon sternly, "you're being unreasonable. Really you are. First you accused me of being
foolish, now you say I did it on purpose. You can't have it
both ways. It's true I cut the plant and I'm sorry. I will re-
place it with a fifteen gallon one immediately."

"You'll do no such thing. All I want from you is to get
off my property and never come back. And don't expect to
be paid for what you've done, either."

"If you mean for pruning your clematis you're right. I
wouldn't think of it."

Jon gathered his tools and dropped them into a large
burlap sack.

"Oh, such impertinence. I never . . . Let me tell you
you've not heard the end of this . . ." She had more to say
but her mouth was so dry she couldn't speak.

At the next meeting of her Community club she presented a resolution that was long on accusations, but short on
its intent; 'to do all we possibly can to get rid of the undesir-

39

ables on the waterfront once and for all.'

The majority of the members were immediately for the resolution and the reluctant ones were too intimidated to speak up. A motion was made and passed unanimously. This would give the club a cause. They needed something, for they were up to here in tea, fashion shows, mild book reviews and colored slides of European trips.

By the time the next city council meeting took place, a committee of five prominent club members had drafted three pages of charges against the houseboat dwellers at Gate 5. The charges were broad enough to cover the entire spectrum of misconduct disliked by a group of women past their prime. Starting with lewd and lascivious conduct, it tempered to immoral and immoderate drinking, dumping raw sewage in the bay, and on down to bad influence on children, cluttering the sidewalks, loitering in the park, and then to economics; i.e. not having much purchasing power and using the library without contributing taxes. It ended with a reference to lazy good-for-nothings, dirty, unkempt, with no pride, and houseboats that looked awful and were a disgrace to the community.

The women could be accused of ignorance as to what constitutes a legal motion, but they'd have to be credited with creativity. Starting with the accidental clipping of a clematis they soon stirred up enough interest to draw most women away from bridge.

The councilmen acted about like all councilmen act when a new piece of business comes before them. They discussed it a while, each member carefully measured his words until he learned how others felt. When it was apparent that a majority didn't care much for the houseboat colony they ordered the building inspector to have the utilities cut off from any houseboat that he felt didn't conform to health and safety standards. They felt good about that one until the city attorney reminded them that Gate 5 was outside city limits.

"Yes. Yes. Well, so be it. Those people out there don't

know the difference. And anyway we have the right to protect the city from a fire."

When news of the council's actions got to Jon he laughed.

"Ha. How sad for them, really. But one can't blame them. They reflect the times, I suppose. You have only to look up there on the highway each morning and evening and witness those locked cars carrying tensions and anxieties to the big city. It's hard to tell which is driven more, the autos or the faces. One wonders where society is going; back and forth, back and forth, it appears from here. But when you think of how those commuters must feel you'll understand why the council acts the way it does. Councilmen are commuters too. They've worked hard for years, and when they go home to their property with financial worries, gastric ulcers and coronary cautions, they pass by here and see us enjoying a beer or a glass of wine. Then they quickly remember that when driving to work in the morning they saw us sitting here relaxing, enjoying, dangling our feet overboard in the mild morning sunshine, drinking coffee from large steamy mugs, slowly letting the day creep in. They are envious, of course, and that hurts. Life has gotten away from them. They've gotten in the position of driving themselves to work for debts, fashions, false fronts and few actual needs. We haven't and they know it. So they've got to hate us. Of course their image of us is warped, for they don't really understand us, nor want to. They believe we are no-good dregs of society, a disgrace to humanity, unambitious, dirty, rude, disrespectful, noncontributors, and by a slim margin too human to shoot. What could be worse? It's true we don't contribute much to the Gross National Product, but what artist does?"

When reminded of the threat to have the utilities cut off, he said that that would never happen. "That's political talk. The council had to make a show and a promise to the women who were present, but it doesn't mean a thing. It

41

can't. It's up to the county. The women, on the other hand, are satisfied with their efforts, and pleased with their elected officials. It will no doubt ride for a long long time and when next mentioned the council will say, 'We're working on it. These things take time. Our city attorney is investigating the law so when we act our action will be legal, forceful and final.' That will be good for two or three months. Later, if asked, the council will say that the utility company's legal staff is looking into it. And everyone knows it can be a long time before corporation lawyers agree on a decision. In the meantime the clematis has grown five feet and will be a better plant than it was before. Mrs. Summers has planned an extended European trip and the other women finally realize that the spirit of community betterment can get watered down, grow weak and piddle away without greatly affecting their lives."

Jon was a constant and ardent defender of Gate 5 people. "What Gate 5 offers to young people cannot be found in any community I know of that is so close to a metropolitan area," he said one day. "Down here we provide the opportunity for young people to rehabilitate, to learn and become competent and useful human beings. I've seen it so many times. The young men and women straggle in, having heard of us, and all they want is a place to live away from pressures and conformity. Most of them know nothing about living, but they quickly learn, make friends in kind, and soon it comes to them they they must have shelter. They look around and see others building and they realize that they, too, can build their own homes. Think of it; to build your own shelter. Where else could they do it? Some are very good and didn't know it, but most are not. Yet to see them working, thinking, experimenting, enthusing, is very heartening. They are learning to become proficient with tools that they had never had in their hands before; how to gather raw materials and make order out of them. I must admit the awkwardness frequently

42

displayed plus the foolish planning and ignorance of basic laws of nature, flotation, winds and forces makes one wonder if they have any sense at all. But, of course, they do. Almost all structures built stand up until the first winter's storm, but I know, and so do others, that they won't last, so we watch and when the destruction occurs, we help salvage, then take them in, and come spring they're right back building again, this time a little better. Soon they have learned to become adept, and really build good shelter. They have gone to school and taught themselves. It doesn't matter that the structures don't conform to a building code. What they're doing is far more important than adhering to some man made rules. For not only have they attained the pride of building their own shelter, but they have learned the value of work, and have provided themselves with the knowledge and confidence in themselves that says 'If I did that I can do anything I put my mind to.' "

Gate 5 has a reservoir of talent. The hill dwellers often hired people from the waterfront to do jobs around their houses: fences, steps, railings, decks and gardens. But there were conditions that went with hiring Gate 5 labor. The most important condition was time. Talent the artists had, but conventionality, organization, schedules, promptness and reliability were not their forte. They could be halfway through a job, and then think of something they'd rather be doing. As Al said one day, "Being gainfully employed is not working for someone else for money. It's working for yourself." Fences could wait. But once the fence was completed there'd be a creative work of art, not just a barricade. Sausalito has many bulkheads holding up massive sides of hills. Most of them are conventional concrete walls, built by commercial uglifiers who, unfortunately, turn out a fast job, and so have more time to move on to repeat the desecration over and over. However there are several bulkheads in Sausalito made

43

of stone, concrete or wood that are a joy to look at. These were mostly made by Gate 5 residents; artists who cared what they were doing to the landscape. Instead of just building, they created and sculptured a lasting wall which was both ornamental and useful, each stone chosen, lifted, and placed in an exact position. But this took time and patience on the owner's part.

Many unusual gardens also have been designed and planted by Gate 5 residents.

Mel was hired by Mrs. Paul to put in a garden. He was recommended by Howard, his friend on the hill. Mel was a capable gardener; just the man his employer wanted for a different garden. The work progressed fast in the beginning. The tearing up, preparation, cans of potted plants delivered, soil brought in, inspiration at a high pitch. Mel enjoyed the opportunity. And then things slowed down, the job half done. Soon it stopped altogether. Mrs. Paul was patient. A month passed. She contacted Howard.

"Has anything happened to Mel?"

"Not that I know of. Why?"

She explained why she called, and added, "He has no phone, you know."

"Yes. I'll try to learn something," said Howard, who felt a responsibility.

Three weeks passed. Howard saw Mel. He questioned him.

"Yes," said Mel, "I really should get on with it. It's taken much longer than I thought it would. I wish I had never started."

"What will you do?"

"I don't know."

"Will you do me a favor?" asked Howard.

"Of course. What is it?"

"You finish that job and I'll never recommend you for another."

Mel was stunned, but understood.

8 **W**hen Jon arrived in Sausalito he had four dollars in his pocket, and felt rich. Sleeping in his car until he found a suitable place to live was not unusual for him. A service station was his bathroom, the library his sitting room. One balmy afternoon he took a walk up Bulkley Ave., saw a path through an unkempt garden and followed it. It led to a cabin overgrown with genesta and other native plants. A closer look told him that the cabin was unused. The closest building was the Alta Mira Hotel. A fence nearby made Jon believe the cabin was on hotel property. Within minutes he had walked down Excelsior Lane to city hall. There he learned who owned the Alta Mira Hotel.

"Do you know this man?" Jon asked the city clerk.

"Oh, sure. Victor Antron. Lives in Larkspur," she replied.

"What kind of a man is he?"

"You don't know him? I thought everybody knew Victor. Besides being a millionaire he owns half the property in this town. Why?"

"I have discovered something important about his property at the hotel. May I use your phone to call him?"

"I'll do it. What is it?"

"Please. It is complicated. I could explain it better. I'll inform him that you allowed me to use your phone."

That satisfied the clerk. "All right. Use that one over there." She pointed to a phone on an unused desk.

Jon dialed and found Victor at home. He explained about the cabin and how he had discovered it.

"Yes. Yes. Could be. I was told there's some cabins down there hidden in the trees. Never seen them myself. Planned to tear 'em down someday and develop the area."

"Until that time," said Jon, "you would have no objection to my living in this one, would you?"

"Objections? Objections? No. Of course not. How much rent will you pay?"

"I beg your pardon?"

"Rent? How much will you pay a month?"

"I wasn't thinking of paying anything. The cabin is unused. I am willing to make it useful. That ought to be worth something, don't you think?"

"Heh! Heh!" Victor replied, amused at the suggestion of free rent. "No. No. I'm afraid that will never do. That is not a business arrangement."

"I know nothing of business," said Jon, "but I do know that I am in need of a place to live and you are capable of providing it. Furthermore I have never paid rent to anyone."

"What?"

"It's true. I think it's wrong to own a roof over another man's head and I never willingly contribute to a wrong. Do you?"

The city clerk and co-worker were fascinated with the

46

conversation. They could only hear half of it, but it was worth double the price of usual conversations. They expected Victor to hang up the receiver any moment, but people didn't do that to Jon. He was polite, amusing, logical and unusual. Most people enjoyed talking with him.

"You are a strange man," said Victor. "Ordinarily I never waste my time speaking to someone I don't know and who has no money. I can't afford it."

Jon chuckled. "Don't worry. I have no fee."

For a man who couldn't afford to talk to a pauper, Victor must have felt in a lenient mood, for he treated himself to twenty minutes of conversation before the two men agreed that twenty five dollars per month would be fair rent.

"You'll have to send me the first and last month's rent, you know," concluded Victor.

"I don't understand," said Jon, "could that mean that the first month's rent shall be the last one I have to pay?"

"It does not. You know better than that."

"Yes," said Jon, "but I was taking the statement literally."

Victor gave Jon his address and the conversation ended. Jon returned to the cabin feeling possessive about it, and within a few hours had moved in. It didn't take long. Three trips from his automobile and the job was completed. He never gave another thought to sending rent money to Victor.

Victor was a busy man. Occasionally during the first few days after the conversation the thought crossed his mind about the strange man who had phoned him. When he had received no rent money he decided the man didn't want the cabin after all.

Five months passed. One day Victor was in Sausalito. He went to the Alta Mira Hotel for lunch. Jon was on the same property preparing his own lunch. Victor saw smoke coming from the lower end of his property. He hastily finished eating and made his way to the cabin. The door was open. Jon was eating and reading from a book propped in front of his plate. He looked up before Victor knocked.

"Good afternoon," he said, pleasantly.

"I am Victor Antron. You are trespassing on my property. You have never paid me any rent. How long have you been living here? I'll get the police. Get out immediately."

Jon remained seated. "I have been here five months. I owe you one hundred twenty five dollars. You shall get it."

"You can be sure of that. When?" asked Victor. His voice dropped in volume as his shoulders dropped a few inches.

"I don't know exactly when. Do you need money?"

"Need money? Silly question. Of course I need money. Everybody does. But that's not the point. I . . . ."

"But it is the point," Jon said, "it's what we're talking about. If you need money you should have it. It's not unusual. Don't apologize. Everybody has their needs." He poured two cups of coffee and invited Victor to have one.

"I'm referring to the money you owe me." He stepped in and sat down.

"Yes, of course. But money is money and you are in need of some. I'm just wondering where we can get it for you."

"You owe it to me."

"I know. But I don't have any. However, a man should have what he needs and I'm willing to help you get it." He faced Victor and appeared to be thinking hard on the subject. "We've all been in situations like this. Sometimes I have to have gasoline for my car. Nothing else will do."

"It isn't that I need money that bad. It's that you owe it to me."

"I see. And it's true I do. But you say you don't need money?"

"Well, yes and no. But it's not right. Damn it, man, you put me in an awkward position."

"I'm sorry you feel that way, for I believe we get our-

48

selves into our own situations. It's easy to blame others."

Victor sipped some coffee. "Damn good coffee. How'd you make it?"

"Hobo. How else?"

"I wouldn't know." He drank some more. "What do you do for a living?"

"Garden."

"Garden? Then you can work for me."

"I beg your pardon?"

"I mean you can pay off your hundred twenty five dollars. I need garden work. Look at this jungle here." He stood up and went to the door. "You've already done quite a bit. Looks nice. You didn't have to do that. Perhaps we can come to some arrangement. How much would you say that's worth?"

"What?"

"What you've done so far."

"A hundred twenty five dollars."

Victor exploded. "That's ridiculous. Now you're being unreasonable. You chose that figure because that's what you owe me. What if it had been seventy five?"

"Then seventy five. You're the one who put value on my work. I hadn't thought of it. There was a need and I saw it. Just as this cabin was a need and you provided it."

"Now wait a minute. Are you trying to tell me that this cabin is equivalent to a little garden work?"

"No. The parallel is that there were two needs. One, the garden, I could afford to do the work it needed. Two, you have told me you could afford to let me live here. You didn't need the money. Perhaps it would lead to better understanding if we didn't put value on our needs."

"You mean exchange?"

"Why not?"

"It's not good business."

"Well, as I've said, I know nothing about business."

"I'm not so sure of that. Oh, dammit. All right. You clean up the rest of this place and we'll call it even. I can't waste any more of my time. Thanks for the coffee."

"You're welcome," said Jon.

During the next few weeks Jon did some off and on gardening around his cabin. Then one day he discovered the Ferry Clementina. It took two days to find the owner. The next day he moved in.

9 Another outstanding resident of Gate 5 was Yanko Varda. Varda was a Greek. A philosopher. A wise man. A friend. A bon vivant. But first and always an artist. When he wasn't painting he talked, sharing his philosophy on life and love and art; to him there wasn't much more of importance. He was an exuberant man of untold age. "I am the only living artist who has had a posthumous art show," he claimed. He had a large, round head, with a tonsure of white hair that contrasted with his tanned skin. Eyes a dark brown that darted about quickly, peripherally, never missing a movement.

51

His accent was as thick as moon dust, his imagination as unpredictable as a bouncing football. An hour with Varda and your mind would reel with stories.

"San Francisco," he said one day, "What an honest city. Where else would you find a phallic symbol so tall, erect and dedicated to the essential? Coit tower. Amazing. And at the base hot dogs. Magnificent."

Varda added a new dimension to Sausalito. He alone could make or break the reputation of a small town. An internationally known and respected artist.

For fifty dollars and a towing charge he bought a huge side wheel ferry that used to ply between Oakland and San Francisco. During high tide he had it pushed onto the spit of land where it rested a bit askew and tender for several years. Occasional high tides washed it farther onto the land, where it finally rested, slowly disintegrating and going back to the sea. Each year finds it settling in the mud, slowly digging its own grave. There's nothing sad about it. The vessel has served its time and usefulness; what better fate does it deserve? To paint and preserve the exterior is showing more respect for the cosmetics than the foundation. For then it would appear alive, but the bones would be weak and tired.

The main deck is two hundred feet long by seventy five feet wide. It used to swallow a hundred automobiles several times a day and belch them onto the other shore without much wear and tear to its innards. This portion of the vessel became the main living quarters for Varda. A few partitions were erected to provide privacy for fussy guests who, in moments of intimacy, felt a bit self conscious. Varda didn't have many such friends, but he built cubicles here and there around the perimeter, made living spaces out of lockers, engine rooms, closets. The kitchen made up one corner of the huge room, with a counter outlining the angles. Benches, beds, cots, chairs, sofas and tables were strewn about everywhere. For a huge, convention-sized room, this one has taken on a

52

lived-in, used and appreciated appearance. There's color every-where. The walls are covered with paintings. Sculpture hangs from the fifteen foot ceiling, or protrudes from the walls. Carvings have been made on the pillars and posts. The floor is nicked and scarred from heavy abuse of autos and trucks, and countless numbers of pedestrians' shoes and boots.

On rare occasions he cleaned his living quarters. There were always several young people around to help.

"Speed is essential," he told them. "Without it you are not American. It is positively not good enough to get the job done; it must be done quickly. If it has to be done again, all right. I do not approve, but that is American. Both must be done with speed. Now then, clear the surfaces of everything. The art will go into this room. What is not art must be thrown away. There will be very little. Attention. I have now made you art critics. Treat your assignment with respect. After that clear the floor of all objects. Put them on the table. This will require judgement. Remember, you are not politicians. Think."

A quick glance around the huge room would depress an army of strong men. There were enough objects to put Porto-bello Market to shame. But with Varda's encouragement the table was cleared first. This took some doing, for it was six feet wide and twenty feet long. Large enough to hold chairs, sofas, beds, small tables, pedestals, sculpture, driftwood, bottles and several unidentifiable objects. Varda talked continu-ally as they worked.

"Ah! Now we will clean the floor. Roger, you will get the hose. The big one. We must do things big. We are Ameri-cans. The girls will take off their jeans, the boys their pants. We are going to swab the floor with oceans of water. Come now, quickly. We must be traditional. It is expected." He handed mops and brooms; attached a nozzle to the hose.

"Varda, what if I don't have panties on?" asked Lor-raine, a shapely young woman, eager to prove it.

"No matter," replied Varda. "We are going to work. What a pity. Freedom of movement, no restrictions, that is essential. Restrictions are for the military. Come, hastily, put garments here. I once knew a man who considered the ultimate intimacy was to listen to the same music as his girl friend. How sad."

The water was turned on, clothes taken off, brushes, brooms and mops loosened the dirt, while the water carried it into the huge scuppers bordering either edge of the floor. The room sang with industry, gaiety, water and laughter. When the floor was cleaned, a rich, abundant odor of wet wood and years of indescribable accumulation filled the room.

Varda was rearranging bottles of various shapes and colors along a twenty foot window ledge. The sun shining through them reflected sparkles of iridescence. It looked at first as if he were playing a useless game of checkers, but when he finished the pattern of shapes and colors made a pleasing work of art. He walked away without glancing back, confident that he had arranged them perfectly.

"Order in art is the only essential," he announced. "If you have made order you have been consistent; that is art. Ah, now we will clear the table and have wine." He picked up a bottle and looked at the label. "We shall try this." After opening it he poured some for himself, and took a mouthful.

"Varda," said Roger, "what's the matter? Is something wrong with the wine? You're mouthing it as if it's so bad you don't want to swallow."

Varda's eyes brightened, then he swallowed, paused and said:

"Not at all. I am tasting it. There is only one way to test wine. I will tell you. Whatever you have heard from the experts you must forget. They tell you to put a small bird's amount into your mouth, to tip the head back, then open your mouth and breathe over the wine adenoidally, asking yourself if the bouquet is right, is the tannin mellowed, how is the flavor, the total acid, to categorize, chemicalize, clinicalize and characterize. I'm surprised they don't suggest you run around in circles like a centrifuge. And then you are to ask yourself: have the acids married well? Now please note, you have not swallowed the wine, and you must not. But who would want to after such torture? Then you spit it out, nod your head knowingly and say, 'Ah!!' exactly as you would in a clinic. It is all such utter nonsense. Remember this, the wine you drink is to satisfy your taste, so don't trust someone else's opinion. Would you ask an onanist what love means to him? No. The secret is this: chew your wine. Take a healthy amount into your mouth, chew it well, push some up behind your upper lip; delicate taste buds are there, chew some more then swallow. Reflect. If it pleases you, buy much, drink and enjoy." He was sitting down. "It is not necessary to sit at the table informally. Unfortunately everyone should dress."

While the scrambling for clothes took place Varda ate some cheese, then said: "The Persians are to be commended. An early race of intelligent people, they taught us to combine pleasure and learning. The multiplication table and intercourse. It was a contest between lovers. Intercourse they knew they could do, not so the mathematics. So they invented the early numbers game to be practiced only during intercourse. It was fashionable to multiply quickly, yet they had a pact, one could only learn it under the pleasurable arrangement. Logic. And so man and woman locked in intimate embrace concentrated on the mental which prolonged the physical. To serve two Gods at one time; Ah, the ultimate." He paused to drink. "But you see," he continued, "all was not good. It tended to encourage slow learners. Some hardly got past the fours, and they didn't care. But worse it made distinctions; it pitted the proficient against each other. And not only that, it made poor mathematicians out of homosexuals. So you see, discrimination is always wrong, always." He stood up, walked to the kitchen and returned with a basket of fruit half as large as a roadside stand. Placing it on the table he said, "Eat, you must eat. Roger, bring more cheese and bread. You are all so serious. Youth. I don't understand you. Come, join me. Pray for my liver. It is of great importance. It should be the first organ transplanted successfully. All efforts should be spent on it. But no, the romantics chose the heart. A pity. One gets a new heart, he must celebrate. But when he does, his liver can't handle it. What a shame."

Varda's living quarters occupied about two thirds of the main deck. The other third was the home of Alan Watts, the philosopher, teacher, Zen master, lecturer, writer and friend of man. Through his writings Watts has probably helped guide more young people toward a meaningful life, and saved them from a futile existence than any man in the 20th century. His writing is clearly sympathetic to the young and at the same time says much for all ages. Dr. Watts almost singlehandedly is responsible for interpreting Eastern philosophy and religion for the western hemisphere.

Varda and Watts liked and respected each other. Both were experts. Watts had a good sense of humor and appreciated Varda's imagination. Living a thick partition away from each other didn't mean they were in one another's hair. Sometimes it was weeks between meetings. Varda worked on his art, Watts deep in writing a philosophical book. Then a chance meeting.

"Alan," shouted Varda, from the gangplank.

"How are you, Yanko?"

"No worse, no worse. Alan, I have a shaggy Zen story to tell you."

"Good. Let's hear it."

Varda would tell a preposterous story fabricated on the spur of the moment. Watts listened attentively, laughing in his loud, open manner. When he finished Varda would say:

"Alan. I am serving lunch in thirty minutes. You will come?"

"Love to."

"Good. And your wife."

"Yes."

Dr. Watts disappeared into his quarters to change from the kimono he habitually wore indoors. Varda continued up the gangplank putting his mind to what he would serve for lunch. It didn't puzzle him long. He was an expert, imaginative, inventive and lucky cook. If it was good weather he would build a fire in a five gallon bucket, set on bricks on his deck. While it burned he sliced veal, and found two packages of shelled peas, gathered the necessary ingredients and returned to the deck. When Watts and his wife came up the gangplank they were met with odors of veal, wine and spices cooking together. They had wine and conversation. The cooked meat was removed and left in the hot, heavy skillet while the peas were placed over the fire. Plates were laid out. By the time the meat was served the peas were cooked exactly right and served hot, firm and delicious. His food was always served on large colorful plates. French bread passed around. Butter, wine. After that came fruit, cheese and a cup of strong hobo coffee. The whole affair took a little more than an hour, then the two men went back to their respective arts.

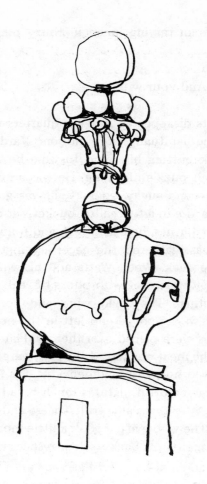

10   In 1950 there were three restaurants in downtown Sausalito. None sold liquor, and only one served beer and wine. They made a fair living, and that was all the owners expected. One such restaurant, or lunch counter, was Jan's, located in a drug store on the corner of Bridgeway and El Portal. The food counter was back of forty feet of glass on El Portal, directly facing the park. Sitting there, drinking coffee, one had a view of the park and more than half of the business district. This didn't mean you had a large, sweeping view, but rather there wasn't much business district to see. But it was a nice place to drink coffee and meet friends, and before you finished a cup you could see who was downtown and where they had been by the packages they carried. Glancing to the right you had an unobstructed view of the Sandspit and the bay. Looking up Bridgeway to the left, you saw the city hall, a clothing store, a butcher shop, a bank, a hardware store, a plumbing shop and the Port Hole. The latter was an institution; a necessity. Its entrance was deceiving, for the door was narrow, and you couldn't see far inside. But once you entered, the walls led you through corridors that branched out into various rooms and closets each stocked heavily with clothing of all descriptions; new, used, abused, mended, fisherman's foul weather gear, work clothes, shoes, boots, galoshes, each with their individual color. It was also a cleaning, pressing and mending establishment. These latter garments after being neatly cleaned and pressed, hung from the ceiling. Ernie, the owner, was a thin, pale man, with a pained smile, always sweatered in navy blue and wearing a green eye shade. He was particular about distinguishing between clothes to be sold and clothes to be cleaned and repaired. In the Port Hole that wasn't easy, but he never lost an article left for cleaning, nor made a mistake. Sometimes a garment hung for years; he didn't mind. His system was simple. Anything hanging from the ceiling was not for sale. And that was considerable. There was an overwhelming number of suits, dresses and overcoats bearing down on you wherever you walked. Ernie's method of serving a customer his cleaned clothes was practical, although a little awkward. After getting identification he'd direct you to stand in a certain spot. Taking a long, smooth, patina-rubbed pole he'd hook the item and serve it to you from fifteen feet away.

Beside wearing apparel, the Port Hole had fishing gear. The bamboo fishing rods standing in a wooden barrel poked

59

up through the alphabetical 'H's' of cleaned and pressed garments. How Ernie ever got those poles inside the store through the maze of crowded corridors was a puzzle. Getting one out was always good for laughs.

Cora, the calm, diligent, dependable lady who did the cleaning, pressing and mending was indispensable to the town. She was always there, standing behind the hissing pressing machine, sitting at the sewing machine or fitting a garment for alteration. The sound of the escaping steam and the odor of damp cloth was familiar to everyone. Some residents after being away for a long period of time would return to say hello and walk through the shop to satisfy their nostalgia.

It often happened that while walking around the store someone would hear a familiar voice. Greeting and a short conversation would occur without the parties seeing each other.

Next to the Port Hole was a plumbing shop. Duke Enos, the owner, was an unusual man in the 1950s; in the 1970s he would be unique. Duke was a plumber who enjoyed sharing the mysteries of his craft with laymen. This didn't endear him to colleagues, but it did to citizens.

The windows of the shop had the usual display of sinks, faucets and fittings, which to Duke were not put there to entice customers, but because it was the safest place to store new and shiny goods. Once up the few steps and inside the shop you quickly learned that order and neatness was not Duke's greatest feature. Scattered over the floor were piles of four inch cast iron tees and ells and closet bends, sections of pipes, boxes of oakum, mounds of lead, plumber's pots and other tools. Overhead, but not far out of reach, were long sections of water pipes, both copper and galvanized steel. On one wall were bins of small fittings, another wall had a long work table showing scars of many years service, stained black from cutting oil. A huge pipe vise at one end with its hardened, intractable jaws and long, smooth handle showed heavy work and dependability. Leaning against the table were various sized pipe threaders. The smell of oakum, hot lead, cutting oil, pipe compound, butane exhaust, coffee, Duke's pipe and a little sweat all marinated together to make a distinct odor of work and material. The hissing plumber's furnace and the ratchety click of pipe threader were familiar sounds to everyone entering the shop.

Besides being an expert plumber, Duke like to help do-it-yourselfers. Residents would bring a faucet to him, and he would carefully take it apart in front of them explaining its workability, laying the separate pieces on the counter in exact order for reverse assembly, and pointing out the flaw: the badly worn or pitted valve seat, poor bonnet packing or stem washer. Then he would watch and direct as the customer reassembled the parts. Duke would get five cents for the washer and a dollar for teaching. More than once he had diagnosed a faulty toilet over the phone and instructed the caller how to make the repair.

What Duke liked best was to teach a novice how to install a whole plumbing system in a house. It didn't happen often, but there were some young people building their homes in the area. They all knew about Duke. When it came time for plumbing a man would bring his blue prints to the shop and while Duke studied them, he'd ask the builder to clear the floor. "Put everything against the walls. We need space," he'd say. Then with a piece of chalk Duke would draw to exact proportions the entire system on the floor, marking and writing in the names of the different joints and fittings. As he talked he taught, sharing secrets and pointers, enthusing, inspiring.

"OK, now draw this on a piece of paper," he'd direct. While this was being done Duke gathered the fittings and pipes. "All right," he'd say, "here's the order in which this should be done." With that he'd place the first piece in position over the drawing on the floor, and mark it number 1. Then the next and so on until it was complete.

"Beautiful, eh? Isn't that beautiful?" To the novice it looked practical, but beauty was not what he saw; he was thinking how good it would be to have it properly installed in his new home. Later there would be more help from Duke. He'd be out to the house to see how the man was doing.

Duke was a soft voiced man, curved stem pipe perpetually puffing from one side of his mouth, heavy set, thick chest filling the blue bibbed overalls, which were worn over layers of other garments. "You never know what you're going to get into," he had said, "it's nice to have insulation when you're crawling on that cold earth under a house."

Duke spent most of his time in the shop. He was a pioneer in prefabricating plumbing. With blue prints at hand he assembled whole walls of pipes that took two men to lift. But it saved many plumbers hours and was a great convenience. He prefabricated out of necessity and for other reasons too. He spent every minute he could in his shop in order to be with his wife. Their apartment was adjoining, but Mary had a desk in one corner of the shop where she could always be found taking care of the accounts, reading, answering the phone or answering Duke. He didn't talk much but when a thought came to him he liked to share it, or check it with Mary. Finishing a hot leaded run he'd stroke it lovingly. "Beautiful joint," he'd say. "Isn't that beautiful, Mary?" "Sure is, Duke," she'd reply.

Jan's drug store lunch counter was the pineal gland of Sausalito. When downtown one always stopped in for a cup of coffee or lunch. If Jan wanted to charge what the coffee was worth she could have made a fortune. But she didn't. She knew how people depended on meeting and talking over a cup and she wouldn't disappoint them by serving a poor brew. All customers were friends. The coffee was rich, strong, made with care and generously served.

Jan was a little under five feet tall and because the stools were up a step, her running back and forth on the duck board floor didn't cut off any view as customers sat, sipped coffee and watched the passing scene, or beckoned for someone to come have a cup.

The park directly outside the windows is a triangular bit of land fifty yards long on Bridgeway. It hasn't changed since it was built in 1920. It has always been bordered with a hedge immaculately clipped in rectangular topiary fashion. Before the park was built the bay water used to slap against rip-rap boulders and kids dove from the curb of Bridgeway for pennies. Then the railroad bought property rights extending far out into the bay, filled the area with earth and laid a bed for tracks. Commute trains from way up Marin County terminated where a ferry slip was built not more than twenty five yards from the main street. So it was the railroad that built the park bordering the tracks. This was not a gift, but a condition. The park stands as a monument to what a municipality can do if the people in power stand firm. After the 1915 Panama Pacific exhibition in San Francisco, some influential citizen in Sausalito acquired two sandstone sculptured elephants the size of a pachyderm foetus and presented them to the city. After the first world war they were mounted on pedestals fifteen feet high on either side of a wide concrete entrance to the park and dedicated to democracy. The connection was vague, as everyone admits, but the symbol was definite. Democrats in town griped a little but acceded in the end. One donkey and one elephant would have looked worse. What the Democrats did was to contribute four avocado trees that have grown up around the elephants. If you look hard you can see baby elephants in the fruit trees. Some old timers have won bets on the scene. It's sobered a few men, also.

The park was heavily used and enjoyed by residents. Baby buggy pushing mothers met in the park, and while children played and romped in the grass, or held sticks against the cascading water falling from a twenty foot high fountain, the women talked and became friends. Many lifelong friend-

63

ships were started in the park by a chance meeting. First the wives, then a dinner invitation where the husbands met and shared interests. Businessmen, too, used the park. Many of them brown bagged a lunch and would sit relaxed in the open air and sunshine while eating a sandwich and chatting with townpeople who happened by.

The pleasures of the park were enhanced by the neatly kept flower gardens bordering the walkways, and the fine trimmed hedge of roses. Mr. Thompson, the gardener, was as proud of the park's appearance as he was of his English accent and heritage. Early each morning he primped and prepared the little park for display with pride and pleasure, then chose a bouquet of fresh flowers for the city hall counter. Residents had great respect for their park and never thought of picking flowers for their own use. Often, when Mr. Thompson cut and trimmed flowers, he gave away bouquets to everyone within sight.

The fountain was encircled by a pool with two or three feet of water standing in it. Occasionally this fountain was used for an unintended purpose. A man named Bart would take a shower in it but not often enough for the people who had close contact with him. Bart was a huge combine of a man, heavily bearded, sprawlingly larded, deeply voiced, and as ungainly as a new born hippo. He was kind, cheerful and his optimism equalled his proportions: large. He lived in a one room shack on the waterfront; his sanitary facility was the tide. He made a living carving wood and selling the result on the street. When sales dropped considerably and townspeople avoided him, Bart knew it was time to bathe. The fountain was the most convenient shower. From Jan's counter the scene was plainly visible.

Bart went about the task in a businesslike way; a job that had to be done for survival. He sat on the edge of the pool and slowly, methodically stripped to his pantaloon type shorts, turned slowly and with the help of his hands, lifted

64

first one leg and then the other to drop his feet into the water. It was cold. Watchers shivered, but not Bart. The thick layers of fat insulated him like a diving suit. The spray made a fine mist that covered his body with tiny droplets. As he stood and leaned his body into the falls he let out groans and grunts, deep harraghs and howls and shouts of glee and awakenings. Then he squirted liquid detergent over his body. It made an inordinate amount of foam; like a soap factory whose overhead sprinkler system unexpectedly let go. As big as Bart was he disappeared inside the flimsy suds that billowed and grew into a huge white cloud of froth. After a few minutes the apparition walked out of the foam, slapping at the clinging bubbles and blindly searching for his towel. The audience cheered. Jan filled a special mug that held a pint of coffee and took it over to him. He gulped it gratefully and dried himself with a huge bath towel.

One day while watching the scene, Gus, a new policeman, saw the strange action. He hadn't been warned, nor was such a scene covered in the police manual, so he thought immediately it had to be a violation. He jumped off his motorcycle and ran through the park, shouting authoritative warnings, to protect the citizen's morals. Bart paid no attention. He was busy. As the huge cloud of foam moved, Gus poked his club at the ghost. Within seconds business houses emptied as owners and patrons rushed into the street shouting at the cop. He withdrew in the face of overwhelming public opinion.

Things evened out at Jan's, or at least she thought they did, and she was boss. Leaving a nickel for coffee and walking away she'd shout at you, "Hey, wait a minute. Cy paid for your coffee yesterday and so did you. Take this." You took it. After a huge lunch of her prize lentil soup and a plate consisting of bright crisp salad, a portion of the casserole of the day, refreshing sherbet to eat with it and maybe a piece of banana bread, you paid, but never left a tip. The place had a feeling similar to eating at home.

Around the corner from the drug store was another popular business: Ray's shoe repair shop. It had a grandmother's house feeling to it; one huge smile. Warm, friendly, welcoming, good to see you, how are you atmosphere; misshaped but comfortable chairs, nostalgic odors, no hurry, no pressure, always-time-to-talk feeling, cookies for children, stronger refreshments for adults, in a back room, newspapers and magazines. Ray was a savior of sorts, even though he dealt in half soles. Citizens always stopped to say hello to Ray when they came downtown. It made them feel better. He handled old shoes with the respect and reverence that curators show fine art. Ray was an artist who could shape a shoe to fit corns and bunions and misshapen feet that brought smiles of relief and wonder to the sufferer. An indispensable man. A shop of miracles.

Lee Chong was not an inscrutable oriental, nor did he have to be to run a good laundry. His shop was a few doors down the street from Ray's. Besides doing the best linen for the finest homes in Sausalito, Lee was a sew, patch and clean artist who kept shirts and dresses in presentable appearance for residents. His philosophy was clear and simple; a piece of cloth brought to his shop was something to be cleaned, ironed and handled with respect.

Another point that distinguished Lee Chong was his method of handling charges. He didn't keep a book of unpaid tickets tucked away in a drawer. Instead he had a large piece of laundry wrapper pinned to the wall on which were listed the names of customers and the amount they owed. This was clearly and publicly displayed on the wall, in the debtor's handwriting for authenticity. Lee, using his stained and stubby fingers on a five wired abacus quickly flicked the discs and mysteriously came up with the sum, all with the confidence of a computer. The customer then wrote the amount he owed after his name if he didn't have cash. When paid in full, a line was drawn through the name. Receipt enough. When the list got messy from too many lines and additions, Lee would start a new list, making the customer write his name and the amount owed. Often the customer would pay up rather than go through with the ordeal. Lee knew this.

Lee often took short vacations with his whole family to the sun and mineral waters of Calistoga. Parking his old but dependable station wagon in front of his shop, he'd load it with special foods and gear. He moved slowly, but with a resolute and determined manner. Everything fitted neatly in place. Next came his wife and children. After all steam valves were turned off, electrical cords disconnected, his last act was to carry his fragile, bald and brittle boned mother to the car and place her in the most comfortable seat. He never announced in advance he was leaving. A party dress would have to hang and wait until his return. A sign in the window told you he was gone, but not when he would return. It stated factually, succinctly, 'CLOSED FOR BUSINESS.'

Every Saturday had a festive atmosphere downtown with no preparation and nothing special to celebrate. But because it was a day of liberation from commuting to San Francisco for most residents, it allowed them to visit Ray, pick up hinges or paint at the hardware store, get laundry, something special from the butcher shop, and then to have coffee at Jan's, and perhaps discuss the latest city council actions. For some residents, mostly men, it was the only time they saw their neighbors. But these casual meetings with Saturday's gossip and business helped hold the town together. Everyone knew each other: their habits, history, peculiarities. If a stranger was seen in town he was a friend of some citizen, and if he was there for more than a day you knew who he was.

A hundred feet from the drugstore on the water's edge was a small public dock. Many residents living a mile north of town made the trip on Saturday in their sailboats. After tying up they'd stop for coffee, then do weekly errands, mainly groceries, go back to Jan's for lunch, then buy wines and liquors at the drug store, board their boat and sail back. It made pleasure out of those weekly chores.

One single minded and determined businessman in Sausalito was Lou Kellam. He owned a butcher shop, had a good business, served his customers well and appeared to enjoy the trade, but an unusual thing happened to him in 1948 that is worthy of recording: he became a vegetarian. For three years after that he continued the butcher business, selling flesh against his philosophy to not eat it. "A man can eat meat if he wants to," he said, and continued honing his knives and slicing through legs and shoulders, necks and backs, eviscerating chickens and hacking off their heads. But the thought of it was getting to him daily, so he started charging higher rates for doing a distasteful task. His customers went along with it for a while, but soon faithfulness fell to the need for proteins. The more his business dropped off, the more Lou enjoyed his life. After he cut through his last liver and sold his last heart, he closed the shop and became the best gardener in town. Almost all his former customers hired him to tend their gardens where he treated plants with the respect and tender loving care a mother bird treats her chicks. Lou thrived in his new profession. For forty years after giving up the butcher shop he could be seen walking the streets with a burlap sack of tools over his shoulder, and a small sandwich in a bag heading for a garden. He died on the job, on his knees, a trowel in one hand. He was 91 years old.

11 across Bridgeway, out of the corner of your eye from Jan's coffee shop, stood the formidable, no-nonsense Jacobs and Krug clothing and haberdashery store. The two men started the store in 1930 and were responsible for outfitting most of the working men of Marin County for more than twenty years. Their location was ideal. It was within fifty yards of the end of the train tracks, and the ferry terminal. Shortly after they set up shop the store became as essential to the working man as his lunch pail. Jacobs and Krug had all grades of clothes to satisfy men in any craft or occupation. It was no wonder the store became a tradition. Off the ferry, a short walk to the store, purchase some goods and take the train home. Pay day evenings the train changed its departure time to accommodate the shoppers. Otherwise there wouldn't have been many passengers. But evenings were the only times the store did any business.

Shortly after they opened, the owners realized they were putting wear on the goods by frequent arranging and rearranging of the counters while waiting for five o'clock shoppers. So they started bringing in children's clothes, some women's apparel, and even tried a few dress clothes for men, to appeal to a different set of customers. The dress suits failed. It was the label that did it. 'Jacobs and Krug. Sausalito,' it read. It was an exclusive that in the 1970s would be a distinction, but in the 1940s it meant nothing. The shopowners were ahead of their time. But they kept trying, and before long they had the reputation they wanted; clothes to fit any need for the whole family. Sausalito was proud of the store and traded there for everything except the most fashionable wearing apparel. A good, dependable store with work shoes and socks, and an odor all its own.

Jacobs and Krug went out of business in 1949. Not from lack of customers, but simply that the owners were tired. It was a great loss to Sausalito. There would be no clothing store left in town.

Jan's for lunch, the Sea Spray Inn for dinner; that was a frequent pattern for many Sausalito residents. The Sea Spray Inn was a family-type restaurant in that nearly everyone eating there knew each other, as well as the waitresses and the bus boys. Every night was like a family get-together with friends, and friends of friends thrown in for variety. But residents didn't come just for the atmosphere, far from it. The food was gourmet in the true sense of the word; wholesome and fresh, with care in cooking and pride in serving. Mrs. Goodale, the proprietor, cook and factotum, had her opinions of how food should be prepared and nothing ever changed her mind. Most important to her was that there were no short cuts. All her gravies, made fresh each evening, were started from browned meat drippings, flour, and water added slowly and stirred continuously into a smooth brown consistency; salt and pepper to taste. Hers. The gravy never tasted the same from night to night for the flavor depended upon

70

the flavor of the meat. It was one of the delights of the restaurant.

The Sea Spray Inn was located on Bridgeway about two hundred yards south of where Ondine's stands. The building was Mrs. Goodale's home, with some partitions removed to make a large room for ten tables, seating four to eight each. She served dinners only from 5:30 P.M. to 9 P.M. The room was well lighted all the time, with a view of the bay if you were near the window. Intimacy was not part of the bargain; dependability was. It was a one fork restaurant that served nutritious food pleasantly in attractive surroundings.

The menu at the Sea Spray Inn didn't have a huge variety. Three of four kinds of meat if the proprietor could find some that was good enough, potatoes, mashed, boiled or baked, never French fried, vegetables in season, some with sauces, but most not, crisp, cold and colorful salads, soup and of course, gravy. Bread and rolls, and occasionally beaten biscuits all baked on the premises. Desserts were mostly puddings or cake. Coffee, but no wine or beer. People ate at the restaurant for sustenance mainly, not for celebrating a special event.

The waitresses were middle aged women residents of Sausalito. Some married, a widow or two. Because they were well known in town there was often an awkward moment when it came to leaving a tip. The custom became ten percent and everyone was satisfied.

Sausalito had a small bakery on Caledonia Street that supplied good breads and wholesome cookies to the residents; and that about tells the story. It was a utilitarian bakery. Their cakes were pleasant, and different from what was baked at home, but they left you with the feeling that you had eaten something that was good for you, instead of indulging in a treat. The bakery did well until Ole Johanson opened a Danish bakery on Bridgeway, and introduced residents to foreign pastry and delights that they had never met before. As Ole mixed, shaped and baked in the back room, his wife served customers and joked about calories and adding a few pounds. That was easy to do. Just standing on the sidewalk looking in the windows and smelling the odors a person could feel the hips growing. It took a stoic to pass by. And this is exactly what Ole intended. His breads alone were a pleasure, but his sweets were sinful and made putting on weight worth all the effort to take it off later.

The first few months Ole worked overtime baking more pastries than bread. And then the situation reversed. He wondered if he had lost his touch, but his wife said he hadn't, she saw the housewives when they came in and noticed the change in their figures, and the way they looked longingly at the treats. In another few months pastry sales picked up; the customers were hooked. Ole kept making the delights. His bakery was a success; customers bought what they felt they shouldn't.

Most small towns have a watch and clock repair shop to keep timepieces running smoothly, but they don't all have a doctor or dentist to keep people in repair. Sausalito had the medics and a horologist. In 1925 Mr. Ellis opened his shop on Princess Street, and for 35 years he kept Sausalitans on time. He was a tall, slender, angular man, humped a little from leaning over his bench, and hardly recognizable without a protruding jewelers loupe in one eye. A dependable, gentle and optimistic man who did more good for the town than any elected official, and was more respected.

The shop was bare and roomy, with display counters on either side, and Mr. Ellis' work table at the back. There he sat behind a high glass counter, a strong light spotted on his hands, his head bent forward peering into the fine works of a watch. Sometimes the low hum of a metal lathe could be heard. He was making a part for a timepiece. When a customer came in he was not greeted with a "Hello, who are you? May I help you?" Everybody knew this. If he jumped up every time someone came in he'd never get any repairs completed. But the moment the customer stepped to the back counter he'd look up friendly and solicitous.

"Could you look at this watch, Mr. Ellis?"

"Certainly. What seems to be the trouble?" He'd reach up and take the watch in his long fingers, then a click could be heard as the casing came off. After a spot diagnosis he'd say, "Can't be much. Next Wednesday all right?"

Watches and jewelry were displayed in the glass counters, all carefully laid out and priced in clear lettering. If a customer was shopping, he or she had only to look around and make a decision. The prices were there. No need to bother Mr. Ellis to ask why one was costlier than another. Residents knew the reason was quality. Mr. Ellis had priced it. If they wished to examine it closely and see it on their wrists or hung about their necks, Mr. Ellis was happy to assist them.

In the late '40s, Mr. Ellis became fascinated with the world of television. To help pass the time and to fill up the large store, he took on a line of television sets; the first in Sausalito. He enjoyed fiddling with the dials, erecting higher and higher antennas, and showing the wonders of electronics to many residents for the first time. When special events were shown, he put a set in the window and within minutes the sidewalk was filled with passersby. Many people hold the memory of having first seen television at Mr. Ellis's.

Perhaps the most joyous, and certainly the most exciting store in Sausalito was the Toy Mart. Henry Malcheski started the store in the building once occupied by the Jacobs and Krug haberdashery. When he opened, he had gone against the advice of his wife, best friends, common sense and a little of his own better judgment. But Henry liked children and Sausa-

73

lito and toys; with a combination like that he said he couldn't lose. If he went broke he'd enjoy doing it. Being surrounded by kids in an atmosphere of harmless fun was, to him, the only way to live.

The Toy Mart was not a mom and dad store where kids could find a few kits, yo-yos, model trains and airplane glue-togethers when they wanted a little amusement. The store had those items, but by the thousands, along with every conceivable game manufactured to satisfy all ages. The only trouble with Henry's store was making a choice. There were magical tricks, stilts, pogo sticks, harmless prank gadgets, chemistry sets, models, puzzles, masks and costumes for all occasions, and on and on and on. And there was Henry in the middle of them all. He was content while pleasing children. "Every day that passes is a day of lost childhood," he maintained. "It's the only time in a person's life for having just plain fun." He proved it. Henry would open any box any time to be sure the child was getting what he wanted. He'd let them play and test mechanical toys after inserting batteries, or he'd wind the spring type until his thumb ached. The store was a wonder of merriment and a bedlam of joy. Children often went directly there after school. Phone calls by the dozens asked if 'my boy was there?' or, 'has Karen come in yet?' The children came to play once more with a tractor or airplane before making a selection. Saturdays they were waiting at the door when he opened, and all day the sidewalks downtown rang with children's feet.

The first day after Henry opened his store he unpacked a large, shiny Wonder Horse, and placed it on the sidewalk outside his door. There the hobby horse sat all day every day, given to the children of Sausalito to ride and dream and entertain themselves. Sometimes Henry would forget to bring it in at night, but it was never bothered. In a short time it became a fixture, dependable and expected. For six years it sat patiently waiting to take on any and all eager children

74

who rocked the daylights out of it to win their imaginary races.

Henry died unexpectedly and his wife Merle carried on the business for a few months until she was forced to give it up. Merle had many offers for the horse, but she declined them all.

"No," she said, "Henry wanted all the children to have it. It's going to the hardware store."

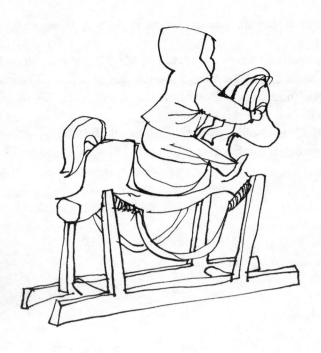

12 **O**ne outstanding business establishment in Sausalito was the Marin Hardware Store. It was situated a half block down Bridgeway from Jan's, on the water side of the street. From the outside it didn't look unusual; two small bay windows, with tools or paint or household goods displayed in them. After 1956 the hobby horse became a fixture on the sidewalk in front of the store. Each morning Mr. Loudon, the proprietor, dragged the horse out and left it all day, without giving it another thought until evening. When his insurance broker warned him of the risk of a lawsuit should a child get injured on it, Mr. Loudon shook his head and said, "Now why would anyone want to do a thing like that?"

76

The hardware store was narrow and dark, with an aisle from the door straight back to the counter fifty feet inside. It was not an easy aisle to walk in, because of the stock cluttering the floor. Mr. Loudon took great pride in this stock and deserved his county wide reputation: "If Loudon doesn't have it, forget it." But storing such a vast amount of material made problems, especially for a small space and a man who had no talent for order. The counters were piled high and precarious with the latest shipment dumped on top. It didn't matter what the box contained. But despite the hodge-podge arrangement the store was a miracle of supply and clerks could always locate a request. It took a little time, but the surprise of finding the item was worth something. And it provided time for a chat.

Mr. Loudon was a huge man, always with a cheerful smile, his head nodding in agreement. His philosophy was simple: satisfy a customer, if there's any profit so much the better. He did an awful lot of business, but not much profit showed on the books. This was mainly due to the number of broken, stepped on, lost or misplaced items. This didn't bother him. His world was hardware, lots of it, and having it available. The measures he took to satisfy a customer were extreme.

Pyrex and other glass items were stored upstairs in a room with no shelves. A hundred or more boxes of various items were strewn on the floor, some spilling their contents, making it an acrobatic trick to walk without stepping on glass. One day a customer wanted the rubber ring from the top half of a silex coffee maker.

"Oh, sure, we have 'em," Mr. Loudon said.

He looked where they were supposed to be but there weren't any. "I'll get one," he said, and went up to the pyrex room. When he came down the steps he was struggling with a ring attached to the top glass bowl. It wouldn't slip off. At the bottom of the steps was a sink. He threw the glass into the sink, breaking it into a hundred pieces, then carefully retrieved the rubber, rinsed it off and triumphantly took it in to the customer.

Everybody in town knew Mr. Loudon was deaf but himself. His stubborn nature wouldn't let him admit it. "I have a little trouble in one ear," he told a hearing aid salesman one day, "but the other one's all right." While this was going on the telephone was ringing violently two feet away.

This attitude showed his stubborn nature. Usually a guessing game preceded the reluctant use of the writing pad.

"I need some light globes."

"Ah. What?"

"Light globes. A hundred watt."

"Ah, paint thinner? Yeah, we have it."

Louder.

"No. Light globes."

"Half gallon? Gallon? Sure, any amount."

The customer shakes his head, then reaches for the writing pad.

Mr. Loudon never thought this was necessary, but he'd shove things aside on the counter, and casually push the pad toward the customer.

Back of the store was an area thirty feet wide and sixty feet long that reached to the water's edge. This wasn't wasted space. It was covered with enough material to prefabricate Grand Coulee Dam, with enough left over to start Aswan. The paint thinner was kept there in a one hundred ten gallon barrel which had a leak. Old timers had a bet on how long it would take for the liquid to cut a runnel to the bay. Seven years it took, which was cheap entertainment.

Other events happened in back of the hardware store among thousands of red clay garden pots, wheel barrows, swollen and split bales of peat moss and manure, buckets, fencing, screen, poultry netting, hardware cloth, baling wire, and other nick nacks. There was an old garden swing facing

78

the bay where clerks from other stores often sat to eat their lunch. It was a sunny and quiet refuge, except for the sea gulls who knew that bread scraps came from people sitting on the swing at that time of the day. In between squawks and rude begging the water lapped peacefully and persistently against the concrete bulkhead. The view of Belvedere Island, Raccoon Straits, Angel Island and passing boats was magnificent. A fine place to relax, eat and build tissue.

The bay water had its drawbacks for the hardware store, as well as its attractions. During extreme high tides the pressure of the water was too much for the bulkhead and the fifty feet of earth to the basement of the store; water seeped in. Not much, only a foot or two, but it was enough to make some of the stock unavailable while the tide was at its highest. When Mr. Loudon first opened the store there was a pump to take care of such emergencies, but neglect had left the pump inoperable. He did the next best thing, laid some planks on top of blocks of wood to walk on, which served adequately if the water was low enough, but a few times a year when the tides were extreme the planks floated. It was touch and go sometimes whether a customer could be satisfied. Brooms, for example were kept downstairs at the end nearest the bay, where deep horizontal racks were built in. It was also the area that got the first water. A dilemma. When a broom was requested, the first thought was the tide.

"I'll see if I can get one," was the reply.

If the water was low the brooms were easily gotten to by tip toeing on the planks, or stepping on boxes of stock. If medium high, this couldn't be done and the customer would have to wait. But if extremely high the brooms floated forward as the water reached the racks and carried the brooms near enough to the bottom of the steps where they could be fished out. A little wiping put them right.

The Marin Hardware store had two clerks beside Mr. Loudon. One full time, six days a week, ten hours a day, another part time. Miss Coan, the full time employee, was as dependable as the tide and complacent as a sleeping puppy. She was also as neat and organized in her mind as her boss was careless in his, but the difference never seriously conflicted with her serenity. Occasionally she'd take a stab at rearranging a section of a counter, but she got no encouragement or help.

"What are you doing that for?" he'd ask.

She'd write a reply. "So I can see what's here."

"Humph! No need to do that," he'd say, off handedly, "just keep your eyes open when you're digging for something and you'd know." He was right about the discouragement, because he knew it was a waste of time. She knew it too, but it offered her a little therapy and cleared a nice place for Mr. Loudon to dump a box when he had to.

Miss Coan's main job was to keep the books and accounts. This was a huge task, for more than half of the sales were charged on a monthly basis. A slip and duplicate was made out at the time of the sale, a copy given to the customer. At the end of the month the slips could easily be added and the amount due sent to the customer, and no one would have doubted it, but Mr. Loudon wouldn't hear of such a callous arrangement. Miss Coan would stack up all the charges for the month for each account, and once more write down on the statement to be mailed, each item purchased during the month, the amount of each item, the date purchased and then total them. All done in neat and legible longhand. A duplication, but a personal touch. Using a typewriter would have been slower because she had but one full arm. Getting out the statements took her more than a week each month, often working after hours, because during the day she was continually distracted by the telephone, interpreting for customers, and waiting on others. Nothing ever disturbed her. She was often interrupted by three requests while trying to find something for someone waiting on the phone and Mr.

80

Loudon calling to her from one end of the store. Her cheerfulness never wavered. A Zen master could learn from her.

Next to the hardware store was the Purity market. This was the only general grocery store in town. Located in a huge, oval topped, corrugated metal quonset building, it had a parking lot next door. The lot is now a public park where exhibitionists perform mostly to laughing sea gulls. The Purity store was well liked. Although it was one of a huge chain of stores, it had a homey feeling to it. It was not large, all the clerks were local, the manager was a native of Sausalito, the butchers knew everybody and all customers knew each other. It was a very important business establishment, and although they had a monopoly in town the prices weren't high because the manager wouldn't be a part of it. The policy at Sausalito Purity was dictated by the manager mainly, and not by a hard and fast rule from Chicago. This was one store where it was safe to say everybody shopped there, although not exclusively. Many people frequented one of the other two butcher shops.

The floor was like an old school room; heavily oiled, dark, worn in places and squeaky. The butcher counter was near the entrance so there was always a trickle of sawdust where you entered, and tracks leading further in. A favorite drinking fountain dispensed icy water that came through pipes within the heavily walled refrigerated meat storage room. Stepping into the store, you were immediately greeted by a friend; customer or clerk. Dotty, one of the veteran clerks, was one of those people who wore a perpetual smile that had a different expression for different people. She was as cheerful as daisies and dependable as gravity. Scotty, the manager, was a large man with thick, black hair that he constantly brushed back from his face. He always seemed to rise up from behind a display counter nearby when you wanted him.

What would be classified as a phenomenon today, was the manner in which the parking lot next to the store was operated. As a matter of fact it was not operated, policed, lined off or attended in any way. Residents used the lot at will, but no one abused it. It's doubtful a fender was ever bumped or a door scratched. It held only twenty cars but it served a thousand a day. The consideration for each other was unwritten and infectious. During the week the shoppers casually shopped and talked a little, but on Saturdays they hurried through, and always with an eye on the parking lot to see if anyone was waiting to get in. No one waited long.

Another grocery store and produce market was across the street from Purity; Bob's Market, owned by Bob Shine and Bob May. Phone orders were a specialty at Bob's. When a call ordered some lettuce, some carrots, some sugar, or whatever, either 'Bob' knew how much of the item to send because of the customer. Any meat ordered they got from Purity as a service. Their delivery boxes were made of hard worn wood strips, held together with heavy twisted wire. The large hand holes were worn smooth and stained from frequent handling. When being stacked in the truck, the boxes had a familiar clacking sound as they came together properly, locked in place. Bob's was the last of the stand-at-the-counter and place-your-order grocery stores. When you finished, the clerk would rush off, nabbing items right and left and be back quickly with an armload of them. Talk and inquire, or commiserate as packaging progressed, then out to the car, placed inside, a thank you, hello to husband, goodbye and close the door safely.

There was no change nor progress made toward merchandising and profit at Bob's Market. But by not introducing new concepts they kept the old tradition of service, consideration and appreciation.

Next to the Purity store parking lot was a rickety old building sitting atop equally shaky pilings. Built in 1920 by the U.S. Navy, it had been used to test communication systems and teach advanced sextant training to officers. The navy abandoned it ten years later, leaving it to teredos, rats, vandals and the elements. Each took its toll. In 1939 a group of women with time on their hands and kind hearts in their bodies, started a Bundles for Britain corps in Sausalito and got permission from the navy to use the old building as headquarters. Husbands cleaned and renovated the structure and the wives started their campaign. Their efforts were successful in collecting a fantastic amount of clothes from generous residents on the hill, and distributing them to the proper agency. After the bundle craze wore off and the British were busy rebuilding their economy and country, the women didn't want to disband, for they felt they had a good group interested in helping other, less fortunate people. A seed was there; they knew that Sausalito had good people, who, when called on for help will respond. Then one of them proposed a Salvage Shop. "If there's clothes to give away there must be other things," she said. There were. The group started the Sausalito Salvage Shop in 1944. It is a one hundred percent charity organization. Women donate their time, and citizens donate the merchandise. Since its beginning they have given $300,000 to various groups. A list of agencies who have been recipients, and the amount of money received, is proudly displayed in the shop.

During the first ten years of their operation in the old navy building, husbands and other handymen fought a running battle with the elements to keep the building usable. But while they were working top side, so to speak, teredos, those sea-going termites, were working on the pilings beneath. The foundation was getting weaker and weaker. Everyone in town was aware of it. A walk on the wooden platform to get to the shop was a test of nerve and daring. Each day the women on duty faced their task with trepidation. Finally the city condemned the building. The women were without a place of business. They knew it was coming, and actually breathed a sigh of relief.

The whole town was alerted. The shop had become a 'must,' a favorite. It took only three weeks to locate another place. In 1958 they moved to their present location on Princess Street, where they continue their volunteer work for charity. A more noble and worthy organization has never been formed. The women who have served their fellow men over the years are heroines.

Brooks was proprietor of the Quality Meat Market, situated across Bridgeway from Jan's lunch counter. Brooks was a large, gentle man, who made a quarter of beef on his shoulder look like a leg of lamb on the shoulder of an average man. His face was big and broad, his hair thick and blond and neatly combed. Brooks had a manner that would gladden the heart of the condemned. His facial expressions and gestures were as wide open and welcoming as grandmother's house on Christmas morning. He moved noiselessly behind the counter, through clean sawdust, carrying a side of beef from the walk-in cooler. The sound of the heavy-hinged door clanking shut was familiar to all customers. Brooks never dropped a piece of meat from his shoulder to the scarred and misshapen butcher block. He had a profound respect for meat. The fear of a bruise compelled him to carefully lay the meat down, and his strength allowed him to. When a customer came in Brooks turned his large head in greeting. His face opened to a special and meaningful smile, his head tipped to one side. Then stepping toward the high display counter he'd wipe his hands on a belt-tucked towel and place them firmly on the counter, slowly turn the palms up, and say, softly, "Hello, Mrs. Miller. How are you?" And his head would tip a little more to one side. He made each customer feel as if he had a special welcome just for them. Perhaps he did. His manner of selecting meat might make one wonder what he chose for another customer, but somehow you felt he saved a select cut for you.

When Mrs. Tew walked into town she received a great amount of respect and attention from pedestrians. If people didn't see her coming their stroll could end in catastrophe.

Mrs. Tew waddled along the street daily from her home in Hurricane Gulch to the business district. Her short, stumpy legs were as solid as barrels and similarly shaped. She had a large head, a flat face and wore glasses as big as a telescope lens and just as thick. The heavy cane she carried was used to flick litter into the gutter. This was an obsession with her, and she went about her task with absolute determination and concentration. This was not a stroll for exercise or pleasure. Nothing that shouldn't be on the sidewalk escaped her eye. Small cigarette butts, matches, newspapers, napkins and sacks. Occasionally she was fooled by the white, slippery splat from a cloacan sea gull. This brought a mumbled curse of her own language. But she kept the sidewalk clear from her home to the hardware store, which was her headquarters. She always stopped there first whether she had business in town or not.

"Eighty seven pieces this mornin'," she'd announce as she entered the hardware store. " 'Tis a shame, tch, tch." Her voice was a hybrid French-Canadian and Yankee, made more fuzzy because her lips moved more from side to side than up and down. "People ought to be nicer than that, eh? A pity."

"Yes," replied Miss Coan, nodding in agreement.

"Do it with me cane, ya know. Push 'em all into the gutter. Terrible. Terrible."

Mrs. Tew's reputation for clearing the sidewalk was legend. There was talk of a city citation for community appearance, but that was quashed when the street superintendent complained that she caused more plugged drains by prodding newspapers into the grids than a winter's worst storm. In ten years of practice she had developed a wrist as strong and adept as an jai alai player's. Sighting a violation, she'd step quickly toward it with one thing in mind; get that paper off the walk. From four feet away the cane lashed out as quick as a frog's tongue and a turn of her wrist flicked the offending scrap into the gutter. Occasionally a pedestrian casually strolling along peacefully viewing the waterfront scene, would get tripped up from a cane between his legs. "Damn nuisance," Mrs. Tew would mutter, referring to the newspaper and hardly noticing the extra resistance. But townspeople knew her and saw her coming. They gave her a wide berth, quickly sitting on a bench and lifting their feet until she passed. If they couldn't make it to a bench they espaliered themselves against the concrete bulkhead like suspect criminals in a raid.

Once a month Mrs. Tew came to the hardware store carrying a large box. As her short legs shifted her body up the narrow aisle, her cane and bulky package knocked pie tins and other cooking utensils off a counter. She didn't hear, for her hearing aid dangled loose from the batteries pinned to her dress.

"Ya got 'ny string?" she asked, "Want to send this parcel to me niece."

Whoever was behind the counter took the package and started binding.

"Tie it good and tight. Ya won't charge 'nything, will ya? Mr. Loudon never does." Then her voice lowered. "Sich a nice man. Don't know what we'd do without 'im."

The clerk circled the box several times with string.

"Wish I could do that. Me 'ands won't let me no more. Arthritis, it is. Painful thing. Shame they can't find 'nything for it. Look at 'em." She'd hang her cane on the counter edge and display her red, swollen hands.

"Too bad," replied the clerk. "Does aspirin help?"

"Eh? To Canada. 'Ats where it goes. Post office won't take it 'less it's tied good and tight. I can't do it no more
86

myself. Used to. It's me 'ands. Clothes they are. For the children. Got 'em at the Salvage Shop. Sich nice things they 'ave there. Did you see me 'at? Got it at the shop too." She'd turn her head slightly.

"Very nice." The package finished, the string cut. "Here you are."

"Thank ye then. They shouldn't have put the post office way out there. Too far for the older folks to walk. A pity." She'd sling her shopping bag over her shoulder, fit her hand into the string, grip her cane, then turn back. "How many pieces did I say?"

"Eighty, I think."

"Eh? Yes, tch, tch. A shame it is." She'd shake her head slowly, pitifully, then start toward the door.

The clerk stepped to the desk to answer the phone. He brushed against Mr. Loudon's arm as he reached.

"The phone? Oh, sure go ahead and use it if you want to."

A short step away from the Chinese Laundry is the Marin Fruit store: better known as Willie's. The store was established in 1919. At this writing it is still in operation. Willie's is the oldest continuous business in Sausalito. The store has served residents faithfully all those years, providing choice fruits and vegetables hand picked by Willie at the produce market in San Francisco. That the store survived economic depressions, fruit failures, crop disasters and tourism can only be attributed to Willie's durability, diligence, cleverness and refusal to compromise. There was nothing inscrutable about it. Dependability was the key. Rarely was the store without the best quality produce. If none was available from the regular wholesaler that suited Willie, he found another source, often traveling miles to attain it. It wasn't always profitable, but it was good business.

Starting with a small push cart, Willie's persistence, help from his family, and support from residents have given him great satisfaction and fair financial rewards. A contented man who has served and been served.

13   The first cultural art center in Sausalito was started in 1948 by Bern Porter. It was located at 579 Bridgeway in one of the gingerbreaded carpenter gothic buildings now occupied by several commercial businesses. The gussied up embroidery on the exterior was added in 1970.

Originally the twin buildings were erected in 1887, one day apart, as residences for parents and son. As the father, Manuel Dinno built one house, the son, who knew nothing about building, followed his father's progress, repeating the identical operation the next day, right next door. When completed, there were two houses exactly alike. The son found

88

the work so fascinating that he became a contractor and built many houses throughout the county. The father had retired from the hard life of sea fishing and sat out his days in the window of his new home watching other fishermen go out to sea each morning and return at night. Not one speck of envy or longing for the old life remained in his body. He had had his fill of narrow escapes, which as a youngster he termed 'thrills,' his long, cold and wet hours of fighting the intense forces of the sea, the cut raw hands from net pulling and salt water, the disappointment of low financial rewards. When the fish were plentiful the price was low. Never a harvest crop: no windfalls. Content in his pride, he puttered around his house forever making improvements. The two houses were examples of utility and honesty in buildings; not one board too many nor too few.

Manuel Dinno occupied his home until 1928. After his wife died he followed her three months later. The son stayed on for a few years, but found Sausalito a dull place to live. He sold the two houses and acquired enough capital to start a construction company. Most tract houses in Novato to the north were built by Manuel Jr. A succession of owners, fore-closers, renters and poachers of the gingerbread houses followed after that. There is no ill wind. A breeze can fan a fire and spread seeds at the same time.

When the opportunity to make a buck at any expense came to Sausalito, along with the tourist trade, there were people to take advantage of it. An enterprising opportunist bought the two buildings in 1970 at a low price and sold them for an outrageously inflated sum. But he had to. He had spent thousands of dollars uglifying and masquerading the honest buildings. That cost, plus profit, inflation and a margin for imagination added up to a reward for disguising historic value. It was wrong; like coloring and adding detail to a 6,000 year old artifact found in a Chinese archeological dig just to satisfy one's personal taste.

When Bern Porter came to Sausalito in 1947 he had only one purpose in mind; art: art in all forms. Porter was not a painter and he was not a pimp or a merchant. He would not take in artists' works and sell them for a profit. His sole aim was to disseminate art. The public should know more about the people who create, he believed, and the only way is to get the artists and the public together. Dialogue, communications, no mysteries, he concluded. He also believed that artists were unselfish and eager to share their talents. How could they be artists otherwise? Porter might have done better had he asked a few artists, but that was not his style. He went into his venture with blind belief. It was an instant success, which, in the art world, means a financial failure. Porter didn't care. He had to live somewhere and he was living. Having been forced into stoicism, he was giving that a good test also. But the artistic community was not being neglected; the opportunity was there. This was not an art gallery; it was a cultural center.

Porter assembled creative people from all possible sources and arranged for them to display or teach and talk on a regular basis. He overlooked no one; priests, mathematicians, physicists, nuns, Buddhists, along with the poets, novelists, painters, sculptors, potters and weavers. All who were thinkers and/or innovators. To Porter there was no bad art; not if it was original. It was the imitators he couldn't tolerate. Varda came and talked color, Enid Foster painting, Mary Lindheim ceramics, Martin Metal toy making. Alan Watts, who was eclecticizing in those days, found an audience. They came, imparted their knowledge to the few patrons who showed up; one or two, then three or four the next week. Double the audience; Porter was encouraged. But the community had been scoured thoroughly, the interested learners enticed from their homes during the first few months. A big night had ten people in the audience. Porter soon learned that residents of Sausalito didn't move to the artistic community because of their interest in art. But he didn't give up easily. A year later he was still plugging away trying to fill a cultural gap.

Porter occupied his quarters for three years. During that time his doors were never locked. The paintings, sculpture and other works of art hanging about were in no danger of theft. People didn't think of locking doors in Sausalito at that time, Porter least of all. A poet or someone with hidden talent who had heard of the cultural center might be in need of a place to sleep; some encouragement. Many mornings Porter awakened to find a stranger or two sleeping on the floor. He respected everyone, took them in, fed and housed them the best he could for as long as they wished to stay. He emphasized hospitality to the verge of hardship. Only in that way, he believed, was the intellect fully awakened and better able to read the laws of the universe. If that were true, any wayfaring stranger who came by had the best opportunity to become a genius. Some of the people Porter helped went on to become outstanding artists who have contributed great works of art. Porter himself became a poet and a publisher. He has written many books and published scores of books by other authors.

After Porter left Sausalito, the center continued for a few years, operated by various artists with egos disproportionate to their talents. But while they were existing in Sausalito, they had a place to dabble and display. Occasionally they'd hang other artists' works and take a commission on anything sold. The cultural art center was out of existence; now it was a gallery. The place went downhill even more to become the present peddler's paradise. The ghost of Manuel Dinno has been ignored and tramped on by so many itinerants who, not ever giving a thought that the houses had a spirit in the beginning, couldn't be expected to recognize one in the end.

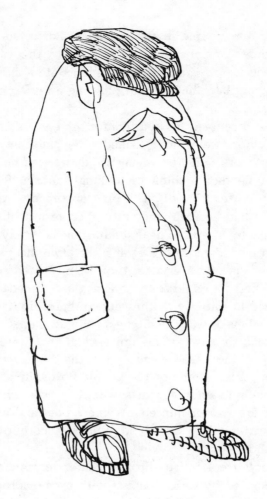

14 **A** mong all the stock out in back of the hardware store Mr. Loudon had fenced an area where he and adjoining businessmen cared for injured sea gulls, ducks, mud hens and other fowl they found around the waterfront. In one partitioned area he could keep cats or dogs brought in from the street, and it wasn't unusual for a child to leave a kitten or puppy he couldn't give away, with instructions for Mr. Loudon to give it to anyone who wanted it. Everyone in town knew about these cages.

Martin, a huge, hard, active man with hands like old blacksmith's tongs, knuckles always scarred, and a voice like the lowest note on a bassoon, lived on a houseboat at Gate 5. Martin looked tough and immovable, but he had a heart as generous as a politician's promises. Let someone be sick in a hospital and he was the first one there with the oranges.

Martin thought and acted in a big way. During a low tide he saw one end of a sunken barge sticking out of the mud. He investigated and learned it was 100 feet long and 50 feet wide. Without hesitation he decided to float her. It seemed an insurmountable task, working under the worst conditions; mud, murk, mess and stink. But he succeeded, and after replacing a few caved in planks he had flotation. Building the living quarters was relaxing in comparison.

In between tasks he often found injured sea gulls or mud hens. Usually they were victims of a cat who, though he got sneaky enough to creep up on a roe-filled gull, wasn't strong enough to kill it. Having knocked the bird off the pier all he could do was look down at the floundering victim and savor some satisfaction for having given the bird its lumps. Martin, hearing the commotion, would grab his skiff and go to the rescue.

One day he had two gulls which he wanted to bring to the hardware store. Martin's only means of transportation was a bicycle. On this day he filled his pipe, lighted it, grabbed the birds by the neck, tucked them under his arms and started the one mile trip to the store. Taking an occasional jab at the handlebars he managed to keep balance and a fairly straight path. He was an excellent rider under normal circumstances, but carrying two sea gulls and a hot pipe which he couldn't attend, was unusual. The gulls, a bit bewildered by it all, seemed to enjoy the attention. They looked about, wide-eyed, with jerky movements of their heads.

During the first part of the trip he didn't encounter many autos and it wouldn't have mattered if he had. He was fresh and nervy and the livestock was calm, although confused. A half mile later this condition changed. The birds, realizing they were being taken for a ride, and forgetting they couldn't fly, tried to anyway. Each effort helped worm their way from under Martin's arms.

"Goddammit," he said, through clenched teeth holding his fast burning pipe, "take it easy, can't you see I'm trying to help you?"

He could have saved his breath as far as the gulls were concerned, and should have for his own comfort. Each time he spoke he fanned the burning tobacco. The pipe by now was a belching inferno. His lips and mouth were hot, his lungs gasping. Fighting the restless birds and turning his eyes from thick smoke, didn't give much time to attend to his steering. By the time he got to the business section of town, the cars behind him were backed up a half mile. Those not able to see what was causing the delay were honking like fury. Directly opposite the small city park, in the center of town, the birds made one last effort and succeeded in freeing their bodies. But Martin maintained his grip on their necks. He tried to swing them back under his arms, but the flapping and beating wings and feet made it impossible. It was all he could do to stay on his own two wheels. Feathers were flying, smoke billowing, horns tooting, people yelling encouragement and Martin cursing the birds, while the entire entourage made an erratic course down the street. When he tried to swing the birds back under his arms it was like trying to contain a couple of helicopters. By now they were dangling by their necks from each handlebar. People up and down both sides of the street were shouting instructions. Shoppers and shopkeepers rushed out to watch the commotion. A policeman shot ahead on a motorcycle and cleared a wide path. Martin kept his balance but said later he lost some poise. The end

94

came a half block from the hardware store. Mrs. Tew, with her cane, was in a pedestrian crosswalk, just having left the hardware store, and saw the strange sight bearing down on her. Half the town was shouting at her to move on, but her hearing aid wasn't working. It would have been but Mr. Loudon tried to sell her a broom instead of the batteries she wanted. When the apparition got close enough, she nimbly stepped aside, then deftly jabbed her cane between the spokes. It gave her a bit of a jolt, but pulling the cane out she humped her shoulders, straightened her lacy bonnet, muttered an unflattering remark about tourists, and walked on. Martin, by a bit of luck and using the spread-winged birds like a high wire artist uses an umbrella, landed on his feet. His momentum caused him to run ahead a few feet before coming to a stop. Then, with regained composure, and a dying need to remove the hot pipe before it boiled the saliva in his mouth, he walked calmly, but hurriedly into the store.

Mr. Loudon looked up as the three entered the doorway, cutting out all light, then turned back to his papers.

Some havoc was created as they moved through narrow aisles lined with precariously balanced tumblers and dishes. Dumping the gulls in the back yard Martin spit out his pipe and doused his blistering mouth in cold water.

One of the characters in town was known as 'The Old Russian,' to many people. Some residents referred to him as 'The Man with the overcoat.' Very few knew his name was George. He led a quiet, private life, and never spoke much beyond a thanks for the food or clothing given him. George spent most of the daylight hours walking up and down Bridgeway window-gazing. He'd stand motionless looking in the window of a real estate office as long as he would at the delicacies in a bakery. Summer and winter his familiar, heavily-overcoated form could be seen silhouetted against glass, as he gazed intently into his own world. George wasn't a beggar, but he subsisted on food from Bob's Market, The Purity, Jan's and the bakery. When he was given something, his hand came slowly out of the deep pocket, received the gift, and disappeared into the pocket again. A warm small smile preceded a barely audible, "Thank ya," his head nodding in gratitude.

George had never been seen wearing anything except an overcoat, which hung to his shoe tops, and wrinkled heavily in the arms from pressure of the cuffs against the pockets. If he suffered from heat or cold, his face never showed it. But every day, in all weather he walked the streets, slowly, effortlessly. As he moved along, his heavily scuffed old work shoes poked their noses out from under the overcoat with each silent step.

Very few people knew where George lived. 'In Old Town, somewhere,' they said. It's true he came from that direction in the morning and returned there in the evening. Neighbors would say, 'Up that street, but I don't know how far.' There was no need to inquire into his private life. He was a harmless old man who never caused any trouble.

One day in 1953 George decided he wouldn't go downtown any more. He had gazed into his last window, nodded to his last friend and benefactor. He had prepared for this. He laid down on top of his bed, fully clothed, hatted and shod. A slip of paper lay on his chest, with scrawly, nearly unintelligible words on it. After it was deciphered, the people who knew him best henceforth referred to him as The Poet. George deserved the honor. He had written his epitaph.

'Bury me in a thin box. Plant a tree over me. If my spirit was weak it won't live, and shouldn't. But my flesh and bones will give life to the tree, housing for birds, shade for lovers. Another spirit will be born, and hopefully a better one.'

15 Sausalito had one fire chief for thirty five years. A good man, always on the job, who could put an everlasting shine on a new chair in less than a week. There was nothing new or innovative about him. Water was made to put out fires, he said, enough of it will do the job. But the town's fire rating grew lower and lower, which made fire insurance rates higher. The chief didn't go for those new fangled gadgets, and argued that they were not only useless, but expensive. 'If you want me to get 'em I will,' he told the council, 'but the budget will have to go up so what difference does it make where the citizen spends his money. Gadgets or fire insurance?' His argument was upheld for years, but when a new council came in, they issued an ultimatum. The chief quit and ran for councilman a year later. His vote total barely exceeded the fire department personnel.

A new chief came in, bringing with him new methods of firefighting and of handling a department. Brick Larson had as much brains as brawn. When he wasn't exercising, he was reading journals on new fire fighting discoveries. In a few months he had whipped the department into shape. It wasn't easy. Getting the men away from the television was the hardest job. After that was pinochle. The men had developed quick wrists from flicking cards, but Brick wanted wrists to swing axes. A few men quit; the sinecure gone. Those who remained quickly learned they had a boss who loved his job.

Brick had much of the nature of a boy scout in him. He was big and proud. In church he stood the tallest, sat the straightest, sang the loudest. He traded on his physical stature. The shorter the person he was speaking to, the straighter and taller he stood. Good natured as a well fed baby, liked a joke, laughed horse-like and deeply, but during training period he was as strict as a special policeman called for his first job. Because he was in top physical condition, he could handle any duty which he expected of his men. The men often bitched about breathing exercises, push-ups, deep knee bends and stationary running, saying that if a call came in right after a workout they wouldn't be able to climb on a truck, let alone extinguish a blaze. But watching Brick lift his knees higher than any of them and more frequently during the last one hundred fast ones, they continued, probably thinking if they were going to drop dead they'd at least have a strong heart.

One day Brick decided to teach his men the technique of rapelling. He called in an expert, a chief from a neighboring town. This man assembled the crew on the roof of the three story fire house and displayed enough equipment to put Sir Edmund Hilary to shame. His enthusiasm was at a high pitch.

"The main fire fighting purpose of this maneuver," he told them as they stood huddled on the roof in a cold, foggy wind, "is that if all ladders are in use and you need to get to a window you can lower yourself on a rope." He never gave them a chance to ask, if all ladders were in use, how would they get equipment and themselves to the roof in the first place.

He dangled a three quarter inch stiff, store-smelling piece of rope, flipping it over casually to show familiarity with the hemp, explaining that rapelling was an old technique used by mountain climbers. He got so interested in explaining technique he forgot a little detail; and would have dropped over the side if a sympathetic fireman hadn't reminded him that one end should be anchored to something. "Sure thing," he said, "that shows you there's a lot to this rapelling and I'm glad you're paying attention." When he finished explaining the theory he was ready to put it to test. Standing on the edge of the roof leaning back slightly, the line taut, he let out enough rope to show how it's done. The men had mixed emotions.

"All right now," he said, "don't be afraid. The important point is having complete confidence. If you know what you're doing you've got control, and with control comes confidence. Right?" He dropped over the side a few feet then stopped. "Notice how my feet are spread slightly apart to keep from twisting. You push away from the building, then when you're away, let out the rope; that's called 'paying out,' then when you come back you'll have dropped further." He demonstrated carefully and successfully a couple of times. Then by sheer strength he pulled himself up and stood perspiring while the men shivered in the wind thinking of hot coffee.

"Now let me show you how fast you can descend if you want to. Confidence, that's what it takes. The further you push out the more you can let yourself down. Use your legs and head. OK. Now watch."

Over the side he went as if he had only two seconds to save a baby's life. "Push out. Give her hell, I could go all the way down in three hitches if I wanted to." He demonstrated leg muscles that would put a high jumper to shame. The second time he dropped eight feet. On the third attempt he would drop further. His knees bent, he shoved, out he went, dangling like a bell clapper, paying out line liberally before swinging in. Unfortunately the city was in good financial condition and money was being spent to paint the interior of the fire house. Smart painters allow ventilation. The window was wide open. The workman was on a ladder. The man was on the end of a rope. He swung in only eight feet from the ground. Two hundred twenty five pounds of determined force went through the open window. Sudden contact sent ladder, paint, painter, brush and dignity sprawling. The men on the roof had seen the chief disappear magically. As they stood looking down, puzzled, the rope moved, then just as magically he appeared dangling in disgust, dripping green paint from his blue uniform. The once bright scrambled eggs on his cap looked bile sick, his fingers gooey with paint worked at the slip knot. Spitting paint he shouted something unintelligible, but the men, halfway between outright glee and restrained laughter, couldn't understand him. The mess disappeared once more, then swung out dispiritedly, dove in and stayed.

16   When Varda decided to have a party he had but to mention it aloud and friends did the rest. It happened once a year, but the event was enough to provide conversation until the next one. These were not ordinary parties. There would be 250 people present; four lambs would be barbequed, dozens of loaves of French bread eaten, bushels of green salad consumed, countless gallons of wine drunk. Just as important were the ancillary aspects such as inhibitions and modesty melted, debauch and dissipation rampant. The unwritten theme of a night on Varda's ferry was acquiesce, agree, approve, concede and comply often; and have fun doing it.

Early in the morning of the party, Steese and a few friends assembled on the beach alongside the ferry. A pit was prepared and a fire started. A half cord of dried oak and madrone was stacked nearby, a huge table of plywood on saw horses erected. One lamb at a time was prepared; first the kidneys were removed, then the lamb copiously salted inside and out and skewered with a ten foot long piece of one inch pipe. Buds of fresh garlic were imbedded in folds of flesh and the lambs were wired in position, stretched full length, legs interlocking. Two lambs on one skewer. A metal frame had been made, with gears and sprockets, motorized to turn the meat slowly over the fire. When the wood had burned down to coals, the lambs were lifted into position and the long hours of waiting, watching, drinking beer, basting, and tending commenced. But Steese had been through the act a few times before and now there was a kind of ritual to follow. It centered mainly around food.

A huge coffee pot was hung over the coals, then the kidneys sliced, potatoes peeled. Long handled black heavy iron skillets were used, veterans of many camp fires. The slightly foggy early morning air was soon filled with the odor of kidneys frying in butter, of boiling coffee and burning wood. It would cure seasickness. When the potatoes were cooked Steese poured in a dozen eggs, stirred gently and let it cook a while longer, then served. As people ate, the lambs turned slowly on the spit dropping juices into the fire.

Varda showed up on his deck in a pair of pink, baggy trousers, with hanging folds of cloth like seaweed on a hawser. He wore no uppers. A soft rope of flesh hung over the belt line. His skin was briar-brown making white chest hair more conspicuous. It took an occasion such as this to get him out of bed before ten A.M. He shouted across the water in his thick accent.

"They are virgin mammaries you are cooking?"

Steese looked up. "Where would we get anything virgin in this town?" he replied.

"Yes, quite right. But wait, I will bring wine. We will celebrate," Varda said and disappeared inside.

But they didn't wait. Dipping French bread in the juices of fried kidneys, followed with strong coffee, was a treat seldom duplicated.

Varda emerged and walked toward them on the long, rickety gangplank. He was wearing a green striped shirt, buttoned wrong, and had slipped his feet into ill-fitting sandals whose heels never left the wooden walk as he sloughed along. His naturally curved index finger was hooked through the loop of a gallon jug of wine, half full. The contents sloshed crazily at each step. Steese had saved a portion of kidney. He sliced it and put it to frying.

Varda joined them, his large face exuding cheer.

"What got you up so early?" he was asked.

"I have extra olfactory perception," he replied, nodding and laughing.

"Varda, for Christ sake," said Steese, "you're going to kill yourself someday if you don't fix that gangplank. It's not safe enough for termites. Why do you leave it like that?"

"It discourages old women," remarked Varda.

"Ha! I didn't think you discriminated about anything."

"It is the gangplank that selects. How unfortunate, for smart women won't come aboard and I abhor stupidity. Yes, a dilemma." He looked about for containers. "Now we shall have wine," he announced.

"It's early to start on that, isn't it?" asked Jon.

"No. The wine is not for us. For the Gods." He rinsed a coffee cup with a bit of wine, threw it away, then poured himself a liberal amount. "Come. There are many Gods; we must not slight any of them." He drank greedily. "Ah, now I will cook." He added a dash of wine to the frying kidneys, stirred vigorously while they steamed and sizzled. After pushing the meat to one side of the pan he added eggs, then salt. "Ah! they are perfect," he said and moved the pan to the table. Breaking bread from a loaf, he ate directly from the frying pan. In between mouthfuls he said: "An appropriate food for early morning. Kidneys. They are what everyone thinks of first."

An hour had passed. Steese walked around the pit,

pushed coals toward the middle, added a piece of wood here and there on the perimeter, sliced a piece of fat from a lamb, stuffed it into a groove of metal-to-metal for lubrication, then sat down with another cup of coffee.

At ten A.M. a truck brought three kegs of steam beer, several gallons of wine, and a five gallon container of barbeque sauce. The sauce was a thick brown-red liquid, heavy with spices and condiments. It was placed near the fire pit. Steese fashioned a rosemary broom made of fresh stalks, bunched together and tied securely to a wooden handle. The sauce was stirred, then Steese thrust the branches into the sauce and wiped the lambs with it, spreading sauce and rosemary flavor. An hour later he removed the cap from a gallon of wine, and swinging the bottle like a watering can, he sloshed wine on the meat sending up clouds of spicy steam. The odor would convert a vegetarian.

Varda had an audience and was holding forth on an endless variety of subjects. He spoke with great authority, but his humor gave him away.

"I performed one miracle in my life," he said, "and of all places, in Los Angeles, but then, it is a city in need of miracles. My best friend was in the hospital. Despondent. Hadn't spoken a word, not uttered a sound for two weeks. Cataleptic. Such a sorrow. And so beautiful. I decided to visit her. One morning I waited for a street car. While waiting I became sick. Poor retsina the night before. Three people were waiting on the bench. I was miserable. Ah, a box. Someone discarded a box. Fate. I opened it. Empty. What luck. I turned away and vomited in the box. Blessed relief. Then set the carton alongside me on the bench. The bus came. I went aboard gratefully. But it didn't last. An honest man who had no inquisitive nature was walking by. He saw the forgotten box, and in one heroic act knocked on the door and thrust the box inside. A passenger pointed to me. It was passed down the aisle. "Ah, yes, how forgetful of me, I said, taking it. I held it an inch above my lap. The bus was crowded. It was hot. Stuffy. The contents beginning to soak through. A long ride. At last my destination. I left the box on the seat as I stepped out. Air. Los Angeles fresh! I walked toward the hospital. I was nearly there. A fresh young girl looking like a large daisy caught up with me. "Mister, you left this box on the bus," thrusting it into my hands. "My mother made me run and catch you. It's leaking a little." "Yes," I said. She kept step with me. "It sure is hot," she said. "I wish I had a coke." A merchant. I thrust a quarter in her hand and she ran back to her mother. I was at the hospital. Many people entering. I looked at the bushes. Moved that way. A doorman saw me. So diligent. He came toward me. I smiled and entered the building with my box. The crowded elevator. Then the corridors. Closets. But no, impossible. Nurses all over when you don't need them. I had no choice. I entered my friend's room. She stared at me. The box. Had I brought her a gift. No. I was ashamed. No flowers. Nothing. A nurse came. "My dear," I said. "This box has valuable and secret contents. Intimate. It must have safekeeping. You are dependable. Please be so good. Guard it with your life while I am here. Can it be refrigerated? It must be. Please." She smiled institutionally and took the box. It was soft on the bottom. Even a nurse would know it needed refrigeration. She left. My friend was so sad. What do you do with your best friend? She had not spoken for 15 days. I was lost. I told her the story of the box. When I finished she laughed. That's it. Laughed so hard and so long it brought nurses and doctors running. When she dried her happy tears she said, 'Varda, you are wonderful,' and she was cured."

He swallowed some wine and while the bottle passed around he was asked what he thought of the new group of artists in the bay area.

"They are wonderful people and buy so many paints. It is good for commerce. Alas! there are no good artists any more. Perhaps some day, but few have painted enough. I was asked to be a judge at a show in San Francisco not long ago. I shouldn't have gone, but I am always hoping. The chairman of the committee begged me to come. 'Oh, I would give anything to have you,' she said. 'Anything?' 'Oh, yes.' Then I met her. A pitiable woman. So old you could only determine her age by the radioactive method. She had nothing to offer that I wanted, or could use. But the show. Shameful. Everyone present was enthusiastic but me. The longer they stayed the more they liked the pictures. But that is to be expected. The champagne put them in a good mood. Alcohol is the artist's answer. The best reviews come from exhibits that serve the most champagne. Perhaps the champagne didn't agree with me, but when I was to judge it was so embarrassing. It was the only time in my life I wished I were in San Jose. I had to speak. 'It is true,' I said, 'that these canvases are strong, they are bold and they are colorful. So all is not lost. If we take all the canvases I see here today and sew them together, they will make someone a good spinnaker.' Then I left hurriedly."

Varda always attracted young people, and he was attracted by them, especially young women. Before the night passed the youngest and most beautiful girls would be vying for his attention. He would have to tell all but one when the time came, exactly as he had several times in the past, 'I'm sorry, but I am dedicated for the night.'

Questions were asked of Varda often, for which he always had a reply, and sometimes the reply came close to answering the query. He was asked what advice he had for young men starting out in the world. Varda looked solemn while his mind turned violently, then he replied:

"None. Absolutely none. I do not guide, and no one should be led. You must have adventure, not certainty."

He reached for wine and everyone knew he would give enough advice to guide a small nation.

106

"A young man should first of all purchase tools. Tools, they are the answer. All tools of all trades. Hundreds, thousands. Hang them on the wall. Look at them every day. Study them. Memorize. Know their use. Admire them if you will, but never, and this is the secret, never touch them. Never. To be proficient with tools means strong muscles and weak mind. You must not learn to do things. Be crafty but do not be a craftsman. A man who uses tools to make a living has handcuffed himself to a life of hard work. He carries a badge of backwardness, he advertises that he knows nothing mysterious. A pity. You must not learn how to make order out of things. That is a mistake. Avoid labor. You must mystify and confuse, like a politician. Inaction, that's the thing. You must be busy producing nothing, for then you are paid highly. Respected. I know men of great disgusting wealth who have their heads filled with strange theories, mysterious obscurities and useless information. They think only in terms of millions of dollars, but when it comes to paying a dinner check they have to ask a guest to count the money. That is practical; they know nothing practical. It is so sad. Our automobile industry. Production line. The man runs back and forth using many tools, carefully adjusting this and that; precisely, quickly, a ballet, so he gets paid nothing. But the man in the office with a desk as big as a heliport; ah! he owns all of the autos. Think. What are the five senses? Your knowledge must ignore them all; then you will be rich. The great chef, a man of essential genius, he performs with his hands, judges with his smell and sight. The owner of the restaurant gains riches and does nothing. Nothing. A promoter makes more than a concert pianist. A bridge designer thinks, a steel worker labors to assemble the bridge in great danger. But the designer's name is on the plaque; credited and rewarded for building the structure." He paused, for only a moment. "It is the same in all professions. Carpenters and architects. Who gets paid the most? Circus performers: Ah, to think that the daring young man on the flying trapeze will only last until he loses his grip, but Saroyan, who wrote the story about him gets paid royalties forever. Writing. Put it in writing. A surgeon can rearrange the mind with dextrous hands and instruments, but he gains his greatest awards only after he has written about it. The psychiatrist who only listens makes more money than the surgeon, the doer. Do not do. Think. Think new. Do not perpetuate monotony, that is what a tool man does; every day the same. A mistake."

"What about a painter, Varda? You do things with your hands?"

"Yes, artists. We are exceptions, and should be. We think and do. But then, artists are not rewarded greatly. Not as much as the art dealer. Never. What is so sad is to know the craftsman is fast becoming a vestigial organism. An oddity. Someday he will be in a wax museum beside the Boston Strangler and mothers will point to the two of them and say to their child, 'Naughty, naughty. You must never become either of those." He stood up and announced that he would go inside and prepare his ferry for the party. Several people followed to help.

It was seven P.M. when Steese decided the lambs were ready. Under Varda's supervision three dozen loaves of French bread had been sliced, countless gallons of green salad prepared, a huge table for carving the lambs set up. Three hundred celebrants assembled in all manner of mood, dress, aims and spirit. When Steese and Jon came aboard carrying two lambs on a long skewer, the loudness of the greetings sent decibels across the bay to San Francisco. The carving was done quickly by several men under Steese's supervision. The meat was juicy, tender and succulent, the salad fresh and tangy, bread sour, drinks abundant. The number of empty wine and liquor bottles could support a small nation by recycling. They were a monument to a successful Varda party. Another mark of success was the variety of dress and undress.

108

This was an opportunity for women to display their imaginations and bodies. Gay garments and headdresses, in unique design, or skimpy mini bikinis more revealing than provocative. Body paints were not unusual, but the heat and moisture made paints run and streak and smear in crazy concoctions. Rivulets of deep purple disappeared beneath a G string, or green film rubbed off a breast by an elbow raised in drinking.

After the lambs were consumed, the party got its second wind. When it ended no one knew. There were no serious casualties, but there were many highlights, mostly private. The few who fell off the deck into low tide and mud only suffered from disgust and ridicule. The effects of the party left men cursing five miles away. This happened when the empty bottles floated with the tide out to the Golden Gate. There were enough to make an invisible band a half mile wide. Early morning commercial fishing boats driving through the fog struck the bottles, breaking them and chipping paint from the hulls like a sand blaster.

If parties are judged by levity and gratification, Varda's parties would rise above their closest competitors by many degrees. The only gravity was its end; for some guests it took days before they made their way down the much abused, rickety, but still durable gangplank.

17 There was other activity besides the tides and the coming and going of ships on Sausalito's waterfront in the early '50s. One such activity was the persistent licking and sealing of countless numbers of envelopes for leftish causes. The scene of this help and encouragement was within two hundred yards of city hall and the police station. Night after night sympathetic friends gathered in the main cabin of the schooner Wander Bird, located in the yacht harbor across from what is now the huge capitalistic complex comprising the Village Fair. There the diligent dreamers of a better society talked and planned and folded leaflets announcing a meeting or another fund raising event. It wasn't hard to find a cause; usually an injustice inflicted upon some depressed or deprived person or persons. This was not an underground movement, although literally it was underwater, for the main cabin was below the main deck, and the ship itself was resting safely, although undignifiedly on the mud bottom at low tide.

110

The workers who gathered on the Wander Bird were not hot headed, conniving communists advocating the overthrow of the government with guns and bombs and violence. They were, without a doubt, the most peace loving and gentle citizens imaginable. They were open and kind, aware, considerate, strongly social minded; the ideal neighbors. If the United States had a form of government that honored people for doing for others instead of doing for oneself, these workers and believers in a better world would be weighted down with medals. They differed from most citizens in their politics; and their politics were not complicated in any way. Nor were they astute political experts. The essence of their belief was simple; the profit system must go. They believed that Socialism was the answer. They could trace every injustice in the U.S. to capitalism. This was their driving force.

Much of their ammunition for criticizing the inequality of the capitalistic system came from the People's World, a newspaper printed in San Francisco. They were as faithful to the P.W. as a financier to the Wall Street Journal. The People's World was an honest and factual tabloid, printing its side of the news just as Fortune Magazine printed its side. The difference was that the newspaper printed faults of the system. Some of the solutions advocated by the People's World have since been adopted by the country as a whole.

Early in the '50s the headline news was the Korean War. Before the U.S. involvement, the workers who came to the Wander Bird printed and distributed countless leaflets advocating that the U.S. not enter the war. When they were unsuccessful in persuading the government to take their advice, they continued with their efforts to get the U.S. out. They never gave up. (Earlier they favored World War II against fascism.) At one time they cursed Truman for going along with big business that got the U.S. into the Korean War, then later applauded him for vetoing the Internal Securities Act. But congress overrode his veto. The act was framed to protect the

111

U.S. against subversive activities such as they were said to be conducting. The group laughed at that. They were supposed to register. No one did. The government would have been smarter if it had enforced gambling laws, because many people thought what kept the movement together throughout the country was the continual selling of raffle tickets to each other.

The Wander Bird had a long history to account for its many nicks and scars of heavy sea travel. She was built in Germany in 1879. Captain Tompkins, his wife Gwen and children, plus a skeleton crew, brought the proud schooner around Cape Horn and on up to Sausalito in 1936. This was the trip for which young Sterling Hayden tried unsuccessfully to sign on as a crewman. Once anchored in Sausalito, the ship never went to sea again. There she remained, a proud fixture, for 30 years. The vessel became the home for Gwen and the children, and a meeting place for willing workers. Captain Tompkins left to pursue other interests.

The Wander Bird got some publicity in 1963 when Sterling Hayden published a book telling of his close association with Captain Tompkins. Mention was made of his communist leanings. Actually Hayden never did much for the party; his communist leanings could better be described as a slight list to the left. Hayden was born with an inquisitive, restless nature, always searching, easily persuaded. Politics was no exception. A talk with the FBI and an appearance before the House Committee on Unamerican Activities straightened him out from whatever minor tilt he had.

Hayden lived in Sausalito in the late '50s. His house was on upper Sunshine Avenue, where he had a commanding view of Hurricane Gulch and San Francisco Bay. But he spent much of his time on the waterfront, working on his schooner Wanderer. Residents never treated him as a celebrity. But many felt a certain pride in pointing him out to visiting friends. Mostly there was an indifferent feeling toward him.

112

In many ways this suited the man.

It was a short walk from the yacht harbor across the parking lot to the No Name Bar. Hayden practically established possessory rights to the path he made going to the popular drinking place.

As an actor, Hayden played his greatest role as himself when he defied court orders and set sail on his ship for the South Seas, taking his four children with him. The year was 1959. One year later to the month a judge decided his action of defiance had reason and let him go with a suspended sentence. Hayden immediately settled down in Belvedere, across the bay, to write the book that was to establish him as a profound writer with talents yet undiscovered. The book proved Hayden to be a modest man; whatever talents he possessed as a writer are still hidden. One interesting aspect came out in the book: whenever he wrote about Sausalito it was consistently his best writing. Perhaps he had more love for the place than he thought. His descriptions were short and accurate and came from the heart.

18 The first large building on the waterfront that visitors see when coming in from San Francisco houses the prestigious Ondine Restaurant on the top floor and the lesser Trident below. This building was built in 1872 as the San Francisco Yacht Club. It replaced a smaller building that had burned. The first yacht club building also served as a meeting place for the town's trustees. It was there that a group of cronies met for the first time in 1893, to start making laws to shape Sausalito. The present building remained a yacht club until 1935. After that it lay idle many years, then in 1945 it became a bait and tackle shop. In 1960 two enterprising ex-seamen, George Gutekunst and Fred Martinez, who had more daring than experience, took over the building and started the Ondine Restaurant. It has been a favorite eating place for the rich cognoscenti ever since. For quality of food it

114

would rate anywhere from one and a half to three stars on the Michelin scale. For popularity it would equal McDonalds.

Sausalito residents remember the building as a bait and tackle shop more than anything else. As a yacht club it was private and stodgy, but as a fishing headquarters it became alive with youth, excitement and usefulness. The building was about the same size as it is now, but its architecture was more severe, plain and honest. It was situated inboard of its present location a hundred feet or so, smack up against the sidewalk, resting on old pilings that were sculptured by weather, worms and weariness. The whole structure was rickety, especially the underpinnings, but somehow it gave the feeling that it would never fall down. It couldn't; for not only was it head-quarters for commercial fishermen, but it was the hub of Sausalito's youth. To children it had always been there, always would be; dependable and indomitable.

The spirit of the shop made it a children's paradise. The owners would take as much time and patience to sell a one cent sinker to a child as they would a thirty dollar net to an adult. Shrimp was the favorite bait for fishing off the old dock alongside the building, and frequently a child would pause and puzzle over buying five cents or ten cents worth, wondering if he should keep some change for a soft drink when the afternoon got hot. Mrs. Barret would wait patiently, then when the decision was made she'd carefully weigh eight or nine shrimp on the huge but tender scales, dump them onto a stack of newspapers and wrap them securely. She had a way of tucking the edges into folds that made string unnec-essary. Children watched the operation carefully, entranced. It was a part of the ritual. Then off through the waterside door to the dock where they joined other playmates. Mothers left children for hours at a time, feeling they were safe and knowing they were enjoying themselves.

What kept the shop in business was the casualness with which it was run. There wasn't much profit, but the attitude of the owners didn't demand it. Besides the bait and tackle for children, commercial fishermen could buy heavy gear of all kinds. Barrels and boxes of shackles, lead weights, chains, rope were set about on the splintery floor, and hanging from the ceiling were nets, poles, anchors, life jackets, and bright yellow foul weather gear. In addition, townspeople would buy fresh fish, whole or sliced. And there was a counter for sandwiches and coffee. Ordinarily you made your own sandwich. Nothing fancy. Loaves of French bread were heaped at one end, some Russian rye and plain American. Salami, bologna, cheeses, and a huge turkey carcass to slice from, roast beef and corned beef. No one paid much attention to the sandwich counter, except for the huge coffee urn. Hot, fresh coffee is as important to a fisherman as proper bait, and the Barrets knew it. Mrs. Barret spent a lot of time out on the dock with the children. Dick, the son, could be busy outfitting a new boat with rope, clevises, stays and other gear when someone wanted a sandwich.

"Help yourself," he'd shout as he walked back and forth dropping line over measured pegs.

"Where's the knife?"

"Damned if I know. Look over there on the bait counter. Or use your own. What kind of a fisherman are you you don't have a knife? Now where was I?" He stopped to look down and count the loops. The knife could be in the oakum barrel, or perhaps left on the cutting board after having chopped squid for bait. The veterans knew it was safer to use their own. The food was an accommodation, not a venture in profit. It started when Mrs. Barret brought a few things down so her son would have a good lunch. It got a little out of hand.

"How much do I owe you?" shouted the sandwich maker.

"Hell, I don't know. What'd you take? You're the one knows. Leave some money on the counter, I'm busy, can't you see?"

116

From the accidental sandwich counter came one of Sausalito's most famous institutions. Dick was spending more and more time alone in the shop, having less time to attend all functions of the store properly. One day a slim, wiry woman came in and suggested to Dick that she be allowed to run the sandwich counter, to which she would add soups and short orders.

"Why?" he asked.

"Well, for one thing people are cheating you."

"Not me. Themselves, maybe."

It was a philosophy she hadn't encountered before. But she explained how she would operate the business and pay him for use of the space. He talked it over with his parents and they said it was up to him. "Go ahead," he told Senna, "pay me what you think it's worth." That was the business arrangement. Within a few weeks word got around that the bait and tackle shop was the best place in town to get soup and sandwiches. What customers lost in informality they gained in quality and sanitation. Never again would a turkey sandwich have the taste of oakum or squid.

Soups were Senna's specialty from the beginning. Her bouillabaise was outstanding. Then one day the latter became superb. Many people believed the fish soup was the best in the bay area. The secret to her recipe came about by accident, flourish and desperation. One old timer, who spent most of his time hanging around the bait shop, gave the following account of how the soup suddenly became so good.

"Dick would go out on a boat to test equipment any time he felt like it, see, and it got so I'd keep an eye on the shop for him. Understand? Yeah. Well the old gal thought she was pretty clever but I noticed that she seemed to have a lot of business around the fish counter when Dick was away. So I snuck a peek one time when she didn't know it and saw her tucking a chunk of salmon and something else in her apron, then tossing it into a boiling pot. I knew she was making

117

soup, you know. You can't fool me. One time she took a few handfuls of bait stuff too, eel, shrimp, some squid and herring. A bunch of third class muck. She had a hellova time cleaning it, but she did and it all went into the soup. People loved it though it made me sick to think about it. I never touched the garbage myself. Of course I didn't tell Dick. I'm not a stooly, understand? And anyway if I did he'd only laugh and say it served the people right for eating in such a dump. Well, hell, it went on until one day she had a big pot boiling and the same thing happened. She had helped herself to a variety of everything, including that bait stuff and she was just beginning to take out the guts and cut off the heads and tails and clean the muck when Dick came back unexpectedly. That tickled me proper. Well the old bat scooped it all up and threw it into the pot without even washing it. It made me sick, ya understand? So you know what happened, don't you? She just spent more time skimming off the muck that boiled to the top, and that's the extent of the cleaning it got. Ach! But she did hold off an hour longer serving her customers and that's the only thing I can say for her. Well anyway, when she did serve the stuff everybody said it was the greatest she'd ever made. I never tasted it myself, see? And I couldn't even keep Dick from eating it. Hell I couldn't tell him why not. So word got around, her reputation grew and her preparation time was cut in half. You never know, do you? Some people have all the luck. Damn, and I never did like that woman."

When the building was bought and moved out to its present location the town lost a fixture, an institution. No longer could a child buy bait and gear, walk the splintery floor, smell the variety, be taught how to fish, or sit on the dock to dream and anticipate. There would be no dock, for how could you allow kids in dirty jeans messing up the area within sight of nine dollar dinners?

In exchange for the bait and tackle shop, and all the

intangibles that went with it, the town got an increase in sales tax dollars from the two bars and two restaurants that went into the building. Sausalito also got hundreds of cars per day that were attracted to the new eating places, bringing with them noise, traffic, pollution and irritation. The children could find other areas and ways to amuse themselves.

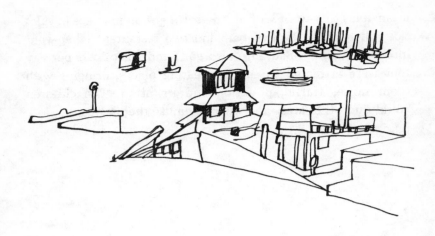

19 The building that now houses the Village Fair was built in 1920 as a garage, storing automobiles in the top floor, with the bottom floor used for a repair shop. It's a historic building, for had it never been there it could never have become gift shops and who knows? Sausalito might never have become the tourist attraction it is. The building was too convenient. Before its transformation the Mason Garage was a huge, square, ugly concrete building built for durability and hard use. It looked like a fortress with only a few small windows to help guide the automobiles up the steep, curvy ramp. Most commuters to San Francisco, before the bridge was built, came to Sausalito by train, but some who preferred the privacy of their automobiles stored their cars in the garage and then rode the ferry where they mixed with the people they had avoided on the train. The ramp used for driving cars to the upper floors is now bricked in as a walkway. "Little Lombard" it's called, a replica of a block-long part of Lombard Street in San

120

Francisco, which is advertised as the crookedest street in the world. Thousands of people a week climb Little Lombard proclaiming it as cute and clever, for it appears that it was designed for its present purpose now used. Take away the bricks lining the path and you're left with a deep scored ramp that used to carry automobiles with unrecognizable names today: Reo, Moon, Hupmobile, Kissell or an occasional Pierce Arrow. All huge, heavy machines with large wheels, some wooden spoked, fenders made of steel as thick and strong as some modern car frames. After the bridge was built, the lower floor continued as an automobile repair shop, while the top floors collected dust and provided a playroom for children who had access through a window with a long plank leading to it from the hill in back. As they visit the shops, long lasting, momentous memories still linger in the minds of some adults, who as children experimented in the area that now houses a bath boutique or a candle stall.

A series of events led up to the present use of the old garage, the forerunner of Sausalito's rapid commercialization.

Next to the steps alongside the Village Fair is the popular liquor store with medical and law offices above. That was a vacant lot until 1960. In the summer of 1949 a man set up a booth weekends in the lot and sold furniture that he designed and manufactured in a shop out in the old shipyard. The residents thought of Luther "Bill" Conover as a good furniture maker who for some reason must enjoy fresh air and sunshine. What other reason could he have for spending Saturday and Sunday in the open air? If they wanted his furniture they all knew where his shop was and could go there to purchase it. Many did. But Bill Conover had a spark of ingenuity that went far beyond designing furniture. Bill was the first person who recognized that Sausalito was a weekend attraction for many Bay Area residents; he did something about his conviction. He was the visionary who gets all the credit or the blame for the town's transformation.

121

The first few weekends in the vacant lot were spent mainly talking to strangers and explaining his furniture's design. A few bought and they told others, and when Bill added ceramics for sale, even the residents purchased from him. The ceramics were 'seconds' from the nationally known Heath Ceramic factory located on the top floor of the Mason Garage. Conover was the first and only retailer of Heath seconds in the U.S. Before that only the prized perfects were available and they were too costly for most people. The seconds were not discards containing misshapen, unfinished or poorly glazed pottery. Most people could not tell the difference. But the inspector could and Heaths had a strict policy regarding their product. Mere off shades of a glaze would not pass muster. Conover's business increased almost immediately. Shortly after that he decided to convert the lower floor of the Mason Garage into a permanent retail shop and move his furniture manufacturing business to the second floor. Heaths would remain on the top floor. Mr. Ross, the garage owner was happy to rent the space and get out of the business. But before Conover could effect his plans he had to get permission from the city for a change of use. That planning commission meeting was a historic one in retrospect. No one at the time foresaw the impact of the application.

The planning commission meetings in those days were a little less boring than present, only because they were shorter. There simply wasn't much going on in town and therefore few applications. On the night Conover's request for a use permit was heard, all nine members of the commission were present. This was unusual in itself, but there was a reason. Just a few weeks before a young, pretty woman began reporting for a weekly newspaper. She sat in the front row taking notes, directly in front of the commissioners. Ann was an attractive woman who, if she wanted to trade on her beauty, had enough collateral to pay off the national debt. She had shapely legs and wore short skirts in the days when they were both noticeable. Because of Ann's presence the attendance record of the commissioners had improved tremendously. Before that it was hard to get a quorum. At this historic meeting, business was humdrumming along at its usual boring pace. It got to be ten thirty when the next item came up. There were only two people in the audience, the applicant and Serge Trubach, asleep. But Serge was always asleep. He found city hall warmer than his rooms. Bob Nissen, the chairman moved to the next item.

"We have here an application for a change of use. Is the applicant present?" he asked. He knew Conover but Bob respected protocol.

Bill Conover said he was present and willing to answer questions.

"What, exactly, is it you want to put in that building?" asked Nissen.

"Well, as you know I've been selling a little furniture on weekends in that vacant lot next door, but now I'd like to move indoors. I'm going to add a few import items also. Not much. That's my wife's interest. The shop will be on the bottom floor, the second floor I'll use for my furniture making."

"So the garage is moving out," remarked Mr. Swan. "Well, he wasn't doing much anyway."

The chairman yawned, and looked around. When no one spoke he said he had no objections. "Does anyone want to make a motion?" he asked.

"What about off street parking?" asked Mr. Thomas.

"What about it?" said Mr. Phipps. "I don't think he needs it. There's always room to park on the streets. A little import shop isn't going to make a problem."

"Not a chance," replied Mr. Starr. "I can't see where he expects to get his customers. We'd probably do him a favor if we refused permission."

"On what grounds?" asked Mr. Phipps. "The area is zoned commercial."

"I know, I know. I'm only saying that an import shop in Sausalito can't possibly make a go of it."

After a little more discussion, none of it more serious than had already been stated, a motion was made for approval, voted on and passed.

Conover thanked the commissioners and left. Serge woke up and followed.

Planning commission actions had to be approved by the city council. There was less discussion among the councilmen than there had been in the commission. Partly because of sympathy for Mr. Conover and his business venture, and because the commission had approved it unanimously. The council rubber stamped the application. In three months the first import shop opened in Sausalito.

For a while there was a little talk around town about the Trade Fair in the old Mason Garage, but generally residents paid no attention to it. Some even thought that maybe that fresh air and sunshine had been too much for Bill's brain. But his modern furniture was selling slowly, as were his wife's Japanese goods. Their experience told them that many San Francisco residents took a little drive on Sunday afternoon across the bridge to Sausalito, where they parked and walked around the quaint little town. Bill stayed open on Sunday. It soon became his best day, but few Sausalito residents knew it. Most were at home. They would be down town tomorrow.

One morning a few years later Bill Conover was sitting at Jan's lunch counter enjoying a cup of coffee. Jan wiped the counter in front of Bill.

"Somebody told me you stay open on Sundays. That true?"

"Sure is, Jan. Been doing it quite a while now."

"I've never been down town on Sunday. Can't picture how the town looks. Wouldn't think there's anyone around." She spooned a bit of potato salad, tasted, approved and tossed the spoon into the sink.

124

"You'd be surprised, Jan. Since I started opening on Sunday I've noticed more and more people on the streets. Strangers mostly. But what surprised me more than anything was a sightseeing bus on the way to Muir Woods. It stopped right over there by the park. Everyone got out, looked around a little, took pictures then got in and the bus left. I got thinking about that so I put a little sign saying 'Souvenirs' and by gosh the next Sunday more than half the people from the bus came to the shop."

"Whadya know?" remarked Jan, and left to serve a customer.

The conversation was overheard by Larry Cox. He hurried home to tell his wife. "There it was staring us in the face all the time. If the sightseeing buses are beginning to stop here they're bringing people, and people buy, especially tourists. And what's more, the bus driver recognizes Sausalito as an unusual place to see and visit. Now it's up to us to give those people something more to buy."

"All right. All right. But what do you have in mind?"

"That whole garage. Can't you see? We'll make shops out of the entire building. Imports from all over the world. It's three stories high. I can see it now. Take that ramp where the cars used to corkscrew up. I'll line it with bricks into a winding path for people to walk all the way to the top. And with your ideas of decorating we can make a showplace. A circus, a carnival. No, a fair. That's it. A Village Fair. Can't you see it? If we had something like that there'd be more sightseeing buses than there are now because we'd be providing something different."

He talked fast, thought faster and enthused at breakneck speed. But by tightening her confidence in his ideas she loosened her purse strings; the purse had been fattened by a legacy of a quarter million dollars.

There was one important detail to be cleared up before the dream became a reality: space. Heath's ceramics had the top floor, Conover's furniture making shop the second, and the retail store the bottom floor. Larry Cox's dream was a 'what if?' If he had the whole building he could make shops. He settled for the next best. It was no secret that Conover had cut down on making furniture. He said his operation was small to start with and he found he was paying high prices for plywood to cut up and glue back together when he could buy the shapes he wanted at less money. So he gave up the shop, sublet it, and concentrated solely on making a go of the free enterprise system: buy cheap and sell dear. He wouldn't mind the competition, for he had other plans.

Getting city approval for the shops was no problem. The area was zoned commercial and Conover's shop had set a precedent. The presentation Cox made to the planning commission and later to the city council was grandiose and optimistic. A few of the city fathers thought the idea was foolish. But they made no restrictions, instead they wished him "Good Luck!"

No mention was made of off street parking. Conover's shop hadn't caused any problems, so who could expect a few more shops would?

The staff at city hall saw the approved application the next day. One remarked:

"I remember as a kid we used to sit down there on the sidewalk after the ferry came in and count the number of cars that came out of the garage. It was a game. It's hard to think that that was much fun."

So the second floor got its transformation. Conover remained on the first floor, the ceramic factory on the top. The name Trade Fair remained. Thirty one specialty shops to start with. Before they were finished, twenty of them were leased. They weren't much. Small cubicles here and there and everywhere. Partitions so thin a long nail driven through a wall hung an Afro mask on one end and Mexican beads on the other. A smorgasbord of international schlock. For a while

126

the shopowners had more time to arrange and rearrange their stock than to wait on customers. But the trickle of tourists increased. Many were rich San Francisco matrons who organized excursions to Sausalito to see the shops and have lunch. It was "chic" among the fashionable. But there were other customers, especially on Sundays. With a little inducement from Larry Cox the sightseeing buses increased. Soon all buses to Muir Woods took a side trip to Sausalito. And when those visitors returned home from their trip west they exclaimed to their friends that "you've just got to see Sausalito. It's the cutest little town you've ever seen. And right on the waterfront. Only ten minutes from San Francisco. And the shops. Why, you can buy just anything."

So their friends and neighbors kept the information in their minds, and when they visited San Francisco they went to see if the description was correct. Some may have gone to see if it was wrong. In either case, Sausalito profited in sales tax dollars and business licenses.

But there was more to come. In 1959 Conover bought a huge ferry. This had been his dream for several years. The 'Berkeley' was used in the San Francisco to Oakland run before the bay bridge was built. Getting permission to tie her up at the foot of El Portal Street in an old ferry slip was no problem. It was city-owned property, but no one was against the use. He then applied for a use permit to sell import items from the ferry. A lease was worked out, the conversion made.

The ferry looked natural sitting down there. It aroused memories in many old timers who had mounted the ramp each morning in years past, to commute to San Francisco. Conover did some repairing, but the old slip and ramp had been well preserved. The ferry was a huge workhorse vessel, bulky, stubborn looking and stable. Painted with fresh white paint, it took on life and had a proud, purposeful appearance. It was only a hundred yards from the old Arbordale which was now Jan's coffee shop. Conover brought the name "Trade

127

Fair" with him and "Village Fair" was tacked onto the transformed garage.

For a while residents thought the new business would take all the trade from the Village Fair, for who would shop in little square boxes when they could go aboard a floating ship? No fear. All it did was to create a mad scramble. When three sightseeing buses arrived at one time the people poured out and scrambled around getting their bearings before making a line toward the ship or the shops. "Oh I'm going to save the boat for last," was often heard. But no matter. Tourists visited both before getting back into the buses to exchange superlatives.

Heath's Ceramics built a new factory in the shipyard area and moved out of the old garage in 1960. Immediately conversion to more shops started. Then land was purchased on the hillside in back and more shops added. The Village Fair complex was completed in 1962.

20   In 1950 your author started working in the Marin Hardware store. It turned out to be an enjoyable and instructive ten years of employment. Actually it was a privilege to be in a store that citizens respected so highly. I had been a customer for several years, buying hardware of all descriptions while building my home. When I asked for employment I said that I was acquainted with the store and knew where everything was. Miss Coan smiled and after a few weeks I learned what an outrageous statement that was. Ten years later I still hadn't learned where everything was, nor everything the store carried. Frequently I'd uncover something new to me. So pleasant surprises became a part of my life in the store.

Because of Mr. Loudon's knowledge of hardware and his philosophy, he was an ideal man to work for. He wasn't the kind of employer to be on a clerk's back every minute to see that he was working. To him there wasn't anything more to a store than seeing that customers got what they wanted. "Those stores that have those counters all cleaned up with stuff in nice rows don't have much else," he said one day. "A hardware store is supposed to have about everything there is. You wouldn't have room for it all if you're going to spread it all out so you can see it. A little digging don't hurt no one."

I agreed. It hadn't hurt him. He'd been digging and finding for 35 years. It wouldn't hurt me to do it on weekends. Back of all this, of course, was Mr. Loudon's lack of greed. It was that philosophy that pleased me the most and made the work a pleasure. In a very short time I realized how much the community depended on him and respected him. His reputation was well deserved and tested by time.

One day I was searching for a tank to fit an old kerosene stove and not having much luck. I found some, but they were for more recent models. Mr. Loudon joined me and I wrote down what the man wanted.

"Oh, yeah. I think I have 'em," he said, and went downstairs. While he was looking I made a cup of coffee for the customer and waited on some other people. After a while Mr. Loudon came upstairs with the tank. The model number plainly stamped on it.

"I knew they were someplace," he said, triumphantly.

The customer was delighted.

"They don't make 'em any more," said Mr. Loudon, as he wiped dust and dirt from the brass container. "It's a pretty old model. They changed the style." He was looking and finally uncovered the price he had made ten years before. "Here it is. Yep. I remember when I bought 'em. A dollar and a quarter plus tax," he said, smiling.

"Oh, it must be worth more than that," said the customer. "They're hard to find. They're practically antiques."

I wrote a quick note to Mr. Loudon. He glanced at it and pushed it aside.

"No, no. That's right," he said, "I priced it at the time. Wouldn't be right to charge any more now."

I had learned another lesson.

My main job during Friday and Saturday that I worked, was to repair small appliances. Toasters, lamps, hand irons made up the bulk of repairs, sharpening scissors and knives another part. During the week the articles would come in and Mr. Loudon or Miss Coan would set them on a table in a back room, or on the floor. Too frequently the table got cluttered with other objects. My first job Friday was to clear a place so I could work. When I finished an article I'd price it fairly and set it aside. Frequently Mr. Loudon would come by and ask how I was doing. "OK," I'd say, nodding affirmatively. If I were puzzled I'd write a note of explanation. "You'll get it," he'd say, cheerfully, and walk away. He knew all the widows and pensioners in town. "Tell you what," he'd say, "she hasn't got much. We'll only charge her for the parts." It happened often and set right with me.

Mr. Loudon was delighted to have the hobby horse. Each morning he'd proudly place it in front of the store and often during the day he'd stand at the window smiling in delight while watching a child in an imaginary race over the countryside. Occasionally I'd bring the hobby horse in and check it over, sometimes replacing an eye bolt or a spring, or touching up the paint. Then out she'd go to serve her friends.

Mr. Loudon went to the wholesalers' in San Francisco every Friday afternoon to pick up supplies and special orders. There was no great need for this, except to please himself. The trips started long before deliveries to Marin County became frequent, and he simply continued the habit. It was another personal touch. During the week, if he didn't have an item asked for, or couldn't find it, he'd say, "I'll have one for you Friday afternoon. Yeah, uh huh!" His falling back on the Friday trips provided me with the biggest laugh I ever got in my life.

I was in the back room working on an obstinate toaster one day. Miss Coan was out for a cup of coffee. Mr. Loudon was alone in the store. I could hear conversations, or the phone, and came out to help only when needed. A lady came in, obviously a stranger, for she didn't know Mr. Loudon was deaf. She asked if there was a rest room.

"Ah! What?"

"Do you have a rest room?" she repeated, a little louder.

"Light globes?"

Pause. "A rest room. Rest room," she said, in desperation.

It must have been one of Mr. Loudon's better hearing or guessing days. He thought she said whisk broom. "Ah, no, no," he said, "but if you can hold off 'til Friday I'll have one for you." He turned to his desk and wrote whisk brooms on the want list.

Another service the store offered customers was daily delivery. There was no minimum. Frequently, too, he'd be asked to pick up an order from the butcher or the drug store and bring it along. He was happy to oblige. I think the man liked to be used.

As commercialization continued, with more and more shops after the Village Fair was built, parking meters were installed. This was predictable. The Chamber of Commerce was insistent on it, for they wanted a quicker turnover of customers, and the additional revenue was welcome to the city coffers. At first there were only a few meters, but soon there were more, reaching out from the hub farther and farther, like insidious tentacles. Then the city had to hire a man to attend the meters. They got a good man, honest, strict,

132

ruthless. But he was entirely lacking in public relations and common sense judgement. Jack Gloss was his name, and he wore a badge that outshined his name. Jack had peripheral vision that could spot a red flag on a meter around a corner, and sometimes in back of him. His ear could hear the click of the hand three blocks away. In his first week on duty he got writer's cramp, then he trained himself to be ambidextrous. The city treasury swelled as his zeal increased. Jack set a goal for himself: to increase written citations every day. When he was seen eating a sandwich while patrolling everyone knew he was running behind schedule. His reputation grew rapidly throughout town, and tourists quickly learned there was someone strict on the job. There was no leniency. He was as relentless as the nearby tide. Red means revenue. He couldn't be talked out of a ticket if the sound of the hand was still in the air. He had freon in his veins and made more enemies in a week than Christ made friends in his lifetime.

One day Mr. Loudon was loading his truck for his daily delivery. It was parked in a metered zone in front of the store, the motor running. He had gone back into the store for a handful of dog cookies. There was a delivery to Mrs. Ahrens and her dog would expect the treat. The red hand on the meter flipped down: a violation. Jack spotted the red. In a moment he was there, writing a ticket. A customer just going out the door saw him.

"You're not using good sense," he said, "can't you see Mr. Loudon is getting ready to leave?"

Gloss gave him a look that would curdle onion juice, pulled out the windshield wiper with his familiar twist of the wrist that was giving him an occupational disease, and let it snap on the citation. Without speaking he crumpled the carbon copy, tossed it into the gutter and mounted his motorcycle with the insolent motion of a dog lifting his leg. This upset the customer. He retrieved the carbon copy, and waited for Jack to come back. It didn't take long.

"Officer," he said, stepping up to him, "I'm placing you under citizens arrest for violating the ordinance against littering the streets."

"What? How do you figure?" he asked.

"This carbon paper," he said, displaying it.

"Huh! You think you're pretty smart, don't you?"

"No, not really. I just like to see laws obeyed. Will you come to city hall with me?"

"Sure, why not?"

He locked his motorcycle and the two started down the sidewalk. The customer held the officer's arm. In no time there was an audience. The shoe repair shop emptied.

"What's up?" asked Ray.

"I'm arresting this man for littering the streets," he was told.

"Hot damn," said Ray, and turned back to the store to tell friends.

Jack Gloss was confident. He wore his official grin and acted superior. Word spread. They crossed the intersection to face shop owners and pedestrians lined up to see the parade, all gleeful that Jack was going to face a showdown.

The police chief met them on the sidewalk in front of city hall, and was told the mission. "I have evidence of the violation," he told him, and showed the carbon paper.

"Alright," said the chief, "come inside." He ordered Jack to wait in one room while they went into his office. He explained that making an arrest was a serious act. The customer reminded him that violating an ordinance is also serious. He agreed. "I never thought about those carbons. Neither did anyone else, I guess. We'll have to do something about it. It won't ever happen again," he assured the man.

"But what about Gloss? He broke the law."

"I'll take care of him, don't worry. Like I said, it won't happen again. Tell you what," he said, "from now on I'll make Gloss bring in all carbons, and if he doesn't I'll dismiss

134

him from the force. That way we'll keep him in line and keep the streets clean. Will that satisfy you?"

"And not go through with the arrest?"

"Yes, if it's OK with you."

"You're asking me to show that man consideration? I doubt if he knows what it is. He hasn't got any more leniency than an avalanche."

The chief didn't reply right away. When he did he said in a quiet voice, "Alright, it's up to you. If you want to go through with this we'll have to go up to San Rafael where official charges are filed. We can go now."

"OK. OK," he replied. "I get the point. Just because he's inconsiderate doesn't mean I have to be. But I've got something at stake here. Arresting him won't change him, I suppose, but he should pay for his crime just as all the people he tags have to pay for theirs. How about making him sweep the gutter between Anchor and El Portal streets each morning for a week. A work detail, so to speak."

The chief smiled. "Sorry," he said, "can't do that."

The matter was dropped, but the customer was treated to three drinks on the way back to the hardware store.

Jack Gloss was back on the job in minutes, patrolling the streets and writing tickets to make up for lost time. He never dropped another carbon.

Sausalito's meter minding men have all been diligent and devoted to their job. You might call them fanatics. If they were working piecemeal they would be millionaires. The man who took Jack Gloss's place was a vigorous zealot. Vic seemed always to be around, anywhere, any time, like Mohammed Ali's left in his prime.

One day he discovered an old car parked in the main city lot downtown, and the moment it was overparked he ticketed it. The next day at one minute past the twenty four hours, another ticket. This continued for eleven days. The last few days gave Vic special pleasure because he knew the price of compound violations. After the eleventh day Vic reported the overparked car to his superior. They rightfully marked the tires, and waited the seventy two hours required before hauling it away. Vic added three more tickets during that time. When the truck came to remove the car they opened the window to release the brakes, and to get the registration certificate. Surprise. The car belonged to Vic. Legally registered in his name. A gift from a few local businessmen. But they had failed to inform him.

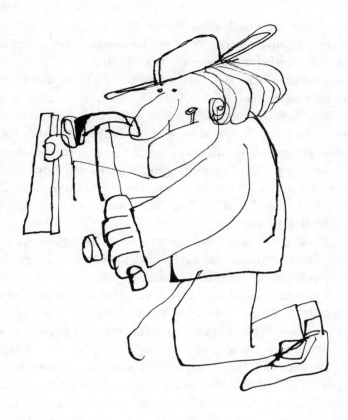

21 The area in back of the hardware store was used
for more than storing stock, keeping injured
animals, teaching a child how to ride a bicycle,
demonstrating how to wire duplicate switches, or
spending a few quiet minutes on the old porch
swing while eating lunch. There was an old building
out there, about ten by twenty feet. The roof sagged
like an old mare's back, and the sunken wood floor
was directly on the earth, eaten here and there by
termites. This shed, or museum, as I like to call it,
was a source of mystery and a miracle of supply.
From the day Mr. Loudon opened the store he

137

started putting supplies out there. He never stopped. And by the time he had covered the floor he couldn't get to the walls to build the shelves he should have built first. If one wanted to get further than five feet inside the door he had to wade over stock two feet thick. Not only was this practice hazardous, but it was highly profligate as well. This was no doubt the reason Mr. Loudon insisted the door always be closed. He felt a little guilty and didn't want people to see his wastefulness.

One day I was in the shed digging through stock looking for a box of porcelain light sockets. Mr. Loudon came out and asked what I was looking for. I wrote a note. He helped dig a little then gave up.

"Tell you what," he said, "I know there's some down there, but they might all be messed up anyway. I'll get some more. Tell 'em we'll have 'em on Friday."

I got interested in the archeological layers of hardware in the shed. When I had time I'd dig away uncovering stock and surprises. What I found told the story of what hardware was selling at a certain time during the 35 years of business. At one corner I found a six foot straight toothed harrow, whose tines had penetrated the rotten floor and were stuck several inches into the ground. On top of this were the remains of cross trees and other harness gear, check hooks, the skeleton of a neck yoke, cruppers, overcheck reins and some black padded blinds. Buggy whips, too, had been thrown in to help bind the mess together. Customers for this agricultural gear, I learned, came from the Alto district just three miles north. Dairies and farms abounded in that area. Now the hillside cow paths are concrete patios. There was other farm gear, sickles, scythes, pick mattocks, Italian hoes. Then at one point there were kerosene lanterns, and a layer of those old gently curved carpet beaters. At one era there must have been an invasion of rats in town, or Mr. Loudon got a good buy and overbought traps. I believe the former, because in the hundreds of traps I found, some were still set, although rusted

138

beyond use. I had to give up the digging when I broke through some tarpaper and released odors and unknown gasses strong enough to melt stainless steel. Underneath I saw decaying leather, broken bottles of pesticides, spilled creosote, hemp rope, oakum and many unknowns. Mr. Loudon said he noticed something rotten out there about ten years before, so he poured a gallon of chlorox on the pile, covered it with tar paper, closed the door for a week and left it. "It helped," he concluded.

An example of Mr. Loudon's hardware knowledge was demonstrated one day when I found a half dozen or more long, multiple curved pieces of wood, with two handles at right angle to the main stock. I'd remembered seeing them in the hands of Father Time on calendars. I brought one out to study it. Mr. Loudon saw me.

"That's a snath," he said.

"Oh."

"A scythe handle. They were the wrong ones. I should have sent 'em back."

"What's wrong about them?" I wrote.

"Left handed," he said, gripping it and demonstrating how a man could cut wheat if it had the blade attached. It was clear that he would have to be left handed.

The herring runs in Sausalito were something to watch and take part in. During the runs the back of the hardware store was a busy place. Mr. Loudon and I were kept busy fashioning makeshift nets out of hardware cloth and rope for children to drop over the bulkhead and haul up the struggling fish. They were literally being caught in the act, totally defenseless doing what they had to do. A fine time to take advantage of them. But Mr. Loudon was right when he said, "It's a good thing they're edible, isn't it? They'd soon take over the ocean if they weren't." So I thought about it and overcame the prejudice while looking at the multitudes in just that small area. I joined in with the children and caught a few to salt down in crocks to leave at the store for people to eat when they had their lunch out back.

The herring continue to come semiannually, but the event is just a show to most people. Up until the late '50s it was strictly utilitarian. Food. Good fresh, free food. All your muscles could pull up in an hour or two. The people who depended upon the fish for a good portion of their diet came with buckets and baskets and burlap sacks and went home with the containers bulging. The waterfront along Bridgeway would be lined solid; wives and helpers in back, the men on the water's edge pulling in the nets, handing them over for emptying. The conditions for herring to spawn were perfect along the mile of waterfront starting at Hurricane Gulch and moving north toward town. The pilings, rocks and bulkheads were what they needed and the first ones the fish encountered after coming in from the ocean. When the herring came they made a fish wave several miles long and a quarter mile wide. It looked as if word had gotten around the entire Pacific Ocean that Sausalito was the place to go. Sea gulls were the first to know. They flew overhead from the bridge all the way in, circling and squawking, heralding the feast and orgy that was about to follow. "What the hell's all the noise about?" the uninitiated would ask. But old timers recognized the sound. They phoned friends on up the county, then reached for their nets and were down at the water's edge when the fish arrived. As the wave of herring got to Sausalito, the females, sensing the appropriate conditions, moved shoreward to deposit their eggs. As the males followed to cover the roe, the fish made a solid blanket. For a hundred yards out the water was a boiling mass. The gulls hovered overhead. When the tide changed and moved out the eggs were exposed and the immoderate gulls moved in to feed on the roe. When filled they vomited the mass and started over again.

GRAND DRAWING!
KPFA

22 One party held in Sausalito in 1959 shook the town almost enough to put an end to future celebrations of any kind in the community. It started innocently, to get a few people together, have fun, and raise a little money doing it. A benefit party for a radio station. This, in itself, was a little unusual, but so were the people wanting to do it. When they got together they demonstrated a spirit of Sausalito that no one knew existed.

The radio station was KPFA in Berkeley; the first listener sponsored station in the U.S., which depended solely on subscribers who voluntarily sent in a few dollars a year to keep it on the air. The station has always been a controversial one and the management is proud of the reputation. When advertisers don't have to be pleased, the policy can be 'tell it like it is.' A number of people in Sausalito liked that kind of broadcasting. The town had more

141

subscribers per capita than any other Marin County community. Some of the subscribers were active and enthusiastic volunteers, giving their time and talents in any way they could. A few of them got together one evening and decided to hold a benefit party for the station. The first question was where? The immediate answer was The Old Town Coffee House. Would the proprietor give permission? They thought so.

Courtland Mudge, the owner of the coffee shop, was a well known, unconventional character about town. He was a tall, stringy man, as easy going as a falling leaf, totally unselfish and as generous as a broken dam. The story is told of him that early one morning he was walking alone on the beach when he spotted an object on the sand. He picked it up and to his surprise discovered it was a roll of five one hundred dollar bills. Mudge looked about him. There was no one in sight. What to do? He had found something he knew wasn't his. Without thinking too hard, he peeled off two of the bills, stuffed them into his shirt pocket, and threw the others down. Asked later why he did that he replied, "Because I'm greedy."

When he was asked for permission to hold the party at his establishment he said, "Of course. Have fun. I'll help at the bar."

The Old Town Coffee House was located on Second Street behind the Jack London House. It was a square, boxy, two story building with more plumbing pipes on the outside than in. Gingerbreaded in carpenter's Gothic, it had the early 1900 look about it. Mudge and his family lived upstairs. There were two large rooms to the coffee house, where if you were lucky you could get a cup of coffee, but first you had to refuse Steam Beer, which was the main item for sale. A handsome bar was installed and two kegs of beer were recessed in cold storage on the wall back of the bar. Tables and chairs of all shapes and designs, furnished by the Sons Of Beaches shop, were set up in a no-pattern pattern. There had never been more than twenty five people in the place at one

142

time. But Mudge didn't mind; he had a place to drink beer with his friends.

The big party was held on a Sunday afternoon. Committee chairmen of various details had organized and planned well, had been on top of everything for days, and were anxious for the big day to prove their capabilities. Food, entertainment, donations of art to be raffled, bartenders, ticket sellers, public address system; everything. And then the skies fell in. Preparations had been made for 75 to 100 people. By mid afternoon eight hundred paid admissions had been collected and people were waiting to get in. The Coffee House suddenly looked very small. It was too crowded for people to move. All tables and chairs had been removed after the first hour. It was stand-up pandemonium, cheerful, cooperative, and joyful. Once inside, the biggest struggle was to get to the bar. Most couldn't, so beers were passed overhead, a few heads sprinkled, money returned. The celebrants were there to have fun and aid the station, so all helped and cooperated in any way they could. "Forget the change. Put it in the pot," was frequently heard. The P.A. system was mainly used to urge people to move about and allow others to get in. As the crowd grew they spilled out into the sidewalk and parking area. People were clamoring to get inside. "They're masochists," said Jon, "but this will prove if they can really take it." When someone made his way to the door and got out for fresh air, his place was quickly taken. If the fire department had been alerted they would have ordered half the people out, and still the party would have been a great success.

In the beginning the food committee tried to accommodate the participants with snacks that had been contributed. But they couldn't keep up. They were running to a store frequently for crackers, cheese, cold meats, but soon they realized it was impossible, uncontrollable. They gave up and helped in other ways. Fortunately the owner of the steam beer brewery opened his doors and sold ten more kegs of beer at cost to the sponsors.

Throughout the afternoon of cheerful chaos four attractive women adorned with large paper roses in their hair, and carrying fish creels strapped over their shoulders, struggled throughout the celebrants selling raffle tickets. Several paintings had been donated by outstanding Sausalito artists: Pankin, Enid Foster, Val Bleeker, Nan Fowler. The announcer frequently reminded the crowd of the raffle and the identification of the women selling the tickets.

"Let the women through, please. That beautiful redhead with the rose in her hair is trying to get over to the music stand to sell someone five dollars worth of tickets. Please pass that money along, will you? Thank you."

The fish creels were stuffed with money. Bill Dempster and Steese at the bar grew weary and were relieved by Will and Poke. Raffle tickets were selling fast. The people who couldn't get inside started a party of their own on the sidewalk. It was gaiety everywhere. The folk singing trio, Carlson, Bratt and Nichols played with gusto, encouraged by the crowd, infected by the enthusiasm.

"At three P.M.," said the announcer, "we're going to raffle the Bleeker painting. Hurry and get your tickets." A mad scramble followed, and a few more hundred dollars collected.

What had started out to be a get-together of a few Sausalito and neighboring KPFA subscribers turned into an unexpected multitude of people with common interests wanting to help the station. It was a hard party to break up, but at 6 P.M. beer sales were stopped and the crowd started thinning out. The money was gathered in boxes and fish baskets, then taken to a home where a few luminaries of the station gathered, along with weary, delighted party sponsors. There the money was dumped onto the living room floor and counted. Twenty-three hundred dollars total. After expenses were paid a check for nineteen hundred dollars was sent to the station. A grand success measured by all standards.

23 Sausalito had its own land grab scandal back in the '40s. But in this case the land had to be made before it was grabbed. Sausalito allowed both. The land we're referring to is directly in front of the Village Fair. It's a flat piece of land, stretching 300 yards into the bay. This is commonly known as the Sandspit. On the end of the spit is the Spinnaker restaurant which was built in 1960. The sandspit looks for all the world as if it has always been there, and in a way most of it was, but it had to be dredged up from the bottom. This was done by Madden and Lewis who owned a quarter mile of waterfront property, which had to be dredged to make a yacht harbor. The area where they wanted to put the spoils was state owned property. The firm got permission and the dredge moved in. As it picked up mud from the bottom, swung and dropped it, the Sandspit was formed. They now had a deep channel for yachts and a windbreak to protect them. But that didn't last. When the mud dried to fine sand and sea shells, and the wind blew strong, the sand started going back to where it came from. So they brought in rip-rap to stop erosion, plus earth from the boring of the Waldo Tunnel, and after a few years they leveled it off and had themselves a sizeable piece of real estate. The city hadn't paid much attention to the project; it was state land, and permission had been granted for the dredging. Then, too, it was on the other side of the railroad tracks. No one in town cared at all what went on out there. If the men wanted to waste their time digging in mud it was their money, their business.

From all appearances the Sandspit was nothing but a waste of bay bottom spoils, sea shells and other dispossessed marine durables, plus the concrete blocks, boulders and other man made rip-rap. High tides often left logs and floating material of all descriptions. Weeds and fennel grew in various places, and kids built forts and bunkers out of available pieces of wood. It was a wonderful place for children to fish from the rocks, to frolic in fun and youthful pursuits. A few years later the joys became more serious. Nearly all Sausalito children at one time or another had experimented in physical love on the Sandspit; it was a campus of vital practical knowledge.

In 1953 the city bought the entire Sandspit from the state, subject to a public trust for navigation and fishing, and leased it to Madden and Lewis.

By 1959 The Village Fair had proven itself. It was attracting people by the thousands, expanding where it could, making more cubicles trying to satisfy customers and providing space for eager shopowners. One day a man and his wife visited the shops, and while she was exclaiming from shop to shop he sat at a second story window drinking coffee. Looking out over the sandspit toward Belvedere, wondering when and where he could eat a lunch, an idea came to him. He'd been in Sausalito many times and never found a good place to eat lunch. "What Sausalito needs is a first class restaurant," he told himself, "and what better location than out on the end of the Sandspit. This is a water-oriented town, so the restaurant should be suspended over the water. I'll put footings on the very end, sink concrete pilings in the water and suspend the building between the two. While the tide slaps away beneath the floor, boats pass by the windows, the customers will take their time eating and drinking and watching the view. Soft music, thick carpets add up to fat cash registers. What a place to wait while the wife does the shops." It was a long conversation to himself but his enthusiasm was up to it. He quickly went to city hall to learn who owned the land.

The next day he talked to Madden and Lewis. Then he spoke with his political friend and partner who came to look at the site, and agreed. Together they started making plans. In less than a week an agreement was made with the firm to sublet the Sandspit. Their plan was for a restaurant, plus shops, a Mediterranean Village. Together with parking it would take up the entire spit of land. But they weren't in business yet. A little detail had to be accomplished: to zone the area to allow commercial uses.

Madden and Lewis and the developers weren't concerned. There hadn't been any organized protests against commercializing Sausalito in the past, and why should there be? The council thought only of the tax dollars that business had brought into the city. It was a businessman's attitude. But they were wrong in this instance. If a commercial value could be put on memories, there would be enough nostalgia attached to the sandspit to balance the budget. In addition there were the beginnings of a new politics in Sausalito. In 1958 a woman was elected to the council for the first time in history. Marjorie Brady was a young, energetic bright woman, dedicated to the old traditions of Sausalito, and concerned about its future. During her door to door campaign she alerted and educated people to the commercialization of Sausalito and as a result she won handily.

At the planning commission meeting Herb Madden, who was spokesman for the firm, and the developers, expected nothing more than making an appearance and answering routine questions before getting approval. After that they could go to the council and get the final go-ahead. Seldom did citizens attend planning commission meetings. There hadn't been any issue of great importance in the past, and because commission actions were only advisory to the council, their decisions weren't taken seriously. But this time was different. Some interested citizens were present and they had questions.

"How much is Madden paying the city for his lease?"

Madden jumped to his feet. "That is not under discussion. We're here to discuss rezoning of an area."

"Primarily, yes, but we would like to know if he plans to sublet the sandspit for more money than he's paying the city."

Madden interposed. "Mr. Chairman," he said, "I think there's some things the people of this town don't know, and I want to tell them. I built that Sandspit. It cost me $20,000 to dredge and fill and bring in bulkhead material. That area down there was nothing but open water with rats, old logs, abandoned boats and debris. I cleaned it up and made something out of it. And now when I have a chance to recover some of my investment there's protests from people who never put up a dime. Mr. Chairman, I've been a citizen of this town for thirty years. I remember when . . ."

He went into his long nostalgic account that townpeople had heard many times before. When he finished a citizen said:

"Mr. Chairman, we're not dealing in reminiscences. We respect Mr. Madden's longevity and faith in Sausalito, but let's not forget that he undoubtedly has already recovered his investment by renting boat spaces in his yacht harbor, while the spoils from the dredging are resting on city owned land. For this he pays a very small amount, and now he wants to insult us by being compensated for the diggings. Ridiculous.

That's double indemnity if I've ever heard it. Most citizens would rather the sandspit remain open space as it is than to have a shopping center on it, with black top, automobiles and traffic. We protest the rezoning application."

Apoplexy got its exercise that night. Mr. Madden replied in a thin, wavery voice: "Mr. Chairman, we did not come here to discuss finances. I think the hearing has gotten out of hand. The planning commission should only consider zoning and uses, not contracts. That part is up to the council."

He was right. But he expected consideration for the amount of money he had spent in building the area. Perhaps some of the commissioners were moved. They played it safe. Their recommendation was to leave it part commercial and part recreational.

This meeting aroused more citizens. A newspaper report divulged the terms of the lease. Perhaps if the developers hadn't been greedy and asked for commercial use of the whole area there would have been less opposition.

Marjorie Brady asked that a citizens committee be appointed by the mayor to study the feasibility of making the Sandspit into a park and buying back Madden's lease and compensating him for his possessory rights. The mayor agreed. A committee was formed. Sam Weinstein was elected chairman. He had an ambitious and dedicated group to work with, and together they sought advice from the state and county officials and the U.S. Corps of Engineers. They got figures from appraisers, lawyers, municipal financial experts and realtors. A thorough investigation.

The developers were getting worried. They went to Madden with a new proposition, one that they thought would set better with the citizens and the councilmen. This was a fifty year lease, which would pay the city $75.00 a month for the first 15 years, then escalate a bit more until 1987. From that year until 2002 they would pay 3% of the gross to the city. And finally to deed the restaurant to the city on the termination of the lease in 2002. Madden would still get his money from subletting the area.

"I wouldn't do it," said Herb. "Let the people yell, it won't bother me. You forget that I built that sandspit. I hold the lease. By rights I ought to be able to do what I want with it." In his mind the construction of the spit equalled the building of the pyramids.

But the developers were afraid that the old lease wouldn't hold up in court. "This one is more lenient," they said, "and gives more to the city. It will set better with residents and show good faith on our part. We're sure some of them will be on our side. We don't want citizen controversy, and certainly not a court test. We have spoken to some of the councilmen and so far they seem well pleased with it."

Herb balked some more, but finally gave in.

When the matter came before the council for final approval the meeting had to be held in a school auditorium. Five hundred citizens showed up.

Sam Weinstein's committee presented a five page report with facts, figures and opinions. For $200,000 the land could be purchased and made entirely into park and recreational purposes and Mr. Madden would get a fair return on his investment. But it would take a lot of persuasive arguments, for the consensus showed the vote three to two in favor of commercial use. The mayor argued the loss of tax revenue. Councilman Ehrlich read the planning commission recommendation, but one of the councilmen objected, saying the commission shouldn't comment unless asked. Boos from the audience. Mrs. Brady begged for more time to allow the people be given a chance to acquire the property if they wanted to. Justin Herman believed a bond issue would win. One councilman didn't speak. Rumors had it that he would get the insurance contract on the property if it was built. The developer outlined a grand plan to have included in the lease agreement. He promised wide open spaces for the public to use, with walks

150

and benches and trees. Places to sit and relax with no sand blowing in people's faces. He concluded with a figure on the tax dollars the business would bring in and how it would lower the tax rate. After three and a half hours of debate a motion was made to grant the application. Just before the vote, Jean Chamberlain rose and shouted in an appealing and accusatory voice, "You're selling out our birthright." And that's exactly what the council did.

Most citizens thought the residents had been taken. But some thought the terms generous, especially the deeding of the restaurant and the planned public areas. What was absent in the agreement was an escalating clause that would have given more money to the city if the restaurant prospered.

While the restaurant was being built the politician applied for a liquor license under a little known state law that allowed a bar license free on land open to the public. The spirit of the law intended the land to be recreational, but by stretching a few interpretations, the Sandspit was declared recreational and the license was granted. It's true that the developers had agreed to make a portion of the area open to the public. There was to be a pathway built along the water's edge, all the way out to the restaurant. There would be benches here and there and the public could stroll along, or sit and view San Francisco across the bay. It could hardly be construed as a recreational area, but if lovers wished to indulge in a little activity who's to say that isn't pleasure? However it never came about, neither the path nor the benches. Little details such as that were left until after the development was completed. And by the time black top roads and parking areas were installed, there simply wasn't room for public paths. No citizen has brought the matter up, and new city councilmen are spending their time on future problems, not bothering themselves with past ones.

24 One morning in 1958 the residents awakened to learn a building was being erected on the east side of Bridgeway across from city hall. This was a complete surprise because that space had been occupied with nothing but unused railroad tracks, rotting ties, and weeds since the ferry went out of business twenty years before. The view of the boats, the water and Belvedere Island was unobstructed from the park to the first old house on pilings a half mile north. The bobbing, weaving ship masts in the harbor were like old friends, and when, on a windless day, sails were hung out to dry they waved a gentle greeting. Driving or walking into town from the north one had a clear view of San Francisco, Angel Island and the Bay Bridge. But now that would all be taken away by the Bank of America, whose sensitivity to the town was blinded by the dollar sign. They erected a hideously plain, square box of zip-zap construction that clearly showed the bank's defiance and the designer's willingness to comply. The only good that came out of it was that the building was so ugly the city ordered evergreen trees planted to obliterate the scene. Having made a mistake in allowing it to be built, the city

152

did what they could to try and hide their blunder. Not until 1974 was remodeling done to make the exterior more presentable. Citizens believed the land belonged to the railroad company. They were wrong, and learned the hard way. Ownership changed hands far too fast for residents to follow, and a fair pace for councilmen who should have known better. It was a shame that any construction was allowed in the area, but the building did serve a purpose. It alerted citizens that a change was happening in their town. Sausalito had been discovered, if not yet by the general public, at least by planners or designers. Had it not been for one fighting resident, all that land would have been privately owned, and instead of automobiles there would have been a solid wall of construction between Bridgeway and the water; a corridor of commerce. How ownership changed hands from a railroad right of way to private ownership is a clear example of the lack of planning and foresight by the city. No one expects councilmen to be prophets, but a little vision is not unreasonable to ask.

It took twenty years for the railroad company to be firmly convinced that the ferries were out of business. In 1957 they offered to the city, for a price, all their right of way land extending from Bridgeway to the water's edge. The councilmen talked it over but because the city had no money at the time with which to purchase it, and no imagination about what to do with the land anyway, they rejected the offer. Parkway Associates bought the land, cleared it, sold the railroad ties and the steel tracks, smoothed the land, then proceeded to sell it lot by lot. The first parcel went to the bank. The building was erected, and while some citizens protested, the developers were busy negotiating with prospective builders for other lots. They sold several of them at a good profit, and held out for their price on the remaining ones. This stubbornness saved the land from development.

At the next council meeting John O'Brien questioned the council:

"How could you allow a building in that location when you must have known it would be contrary to what the citizens want?"

"We couldn't stop it. It's private land, zoned commercial," the mayor replied.

When it was learned that the city turned down the offer to buy the land, John was furious. "You should have known better. The citizens don't want a row of business houses on the waterfront."

"If we had known there was such interest in it we might have acted otherwise," the council replied. "Where were you when we were discussing it?"

"At home," said John, "but last year we were at the polls electing you to represent us. We trusted you to look after our interests. But it appears you don't know what our interests are. We have been fooled. You can't expect us to be down here to speak on every issue. Why have a council if we're going to tell you how to vote? Everyone of you councilmen made a campaign promise to keep Sausalito a quiet, residential town. But now you've demonstrated just the opposite. If you didn't know before, you do now, that that whole waterfront can be a wall of buildings. The bank is just the first. The handwriting is on the wall. You've got to stop it."

The result was a petition by citizens requesting that the city buy all the remaining land. It wasn't a legal tool, but expressing opinions often results in swaying legal decisions. Parkway Associates weren't worried; the land was for sale to any buyer. But when it was learned that some councilmen were against public ownership of the property, another petition circulated asking that the land be re-zoned to prevent commercial development. The owners argued that that would be confiscation of property. But the citizens were getting smart; they knew re-zoning could be done legally. There would be public meetings; both sides would have their day in court. So the council asked the planning commission to study the

154

matter and make their recommendations. It was a needless bureaucratic gesture, but it would get the council off the hook for a while and pass the buck to the planning commission.

The delays and publicity made many citizens aware that their little town was beginning to change, and if buildings were erected on that side of Bridgeway the change would be irreversible. Some attended the planning commission meeting and voiced their opinion. To do this demonstrated great civic dedication, for commission meetings were an exercise in boredom. But citizens who attended learned something about planning commissioners that they hadn't realized before. Because the post is appointive, not elective, the commissioners are usually more objective, more honest in their decisions than councilmen because they never give a thought to being reelected. When there's no toes to step on, a straighter course can be taken. It was not surprising that the commission voted for rezoning: commercial development would not be in the best interest of Sausalito.

In the meantime, the city was negotiating with the owners of the remaining property. When the issue came before the council the public was alerted, interested and informed about the situation. They learned, for example, that it would cost $165,827 to buy the land in question for which Parkway Associates had paid $105,000. It was a fair profit for the owners and not much of a penalty for a city to pay for delays, indecision and learning a lesson. One parcel was owned by a developer from Mill Valley. He offered to sell with the stipulation that the area remain open space. One councilman held out; he was vehemently against the city getting into the real estate business. Mayor Goshen argued for purchase. "It's the opportunity of a lifetime," he said. He was right. The city paid $165,827 for the land and it turned out to be the most profitable business transaction in the city's history. Three years later the entire area was turned into parking lots. Tourists contribute thousands of dollars annually to the city's coffers from those lots. The revenue can go up any time the city decides, and they do this frequently. Automobiles are big business in Sausalito. They're also a big problem. With only one narrow street leading in and out, traffic, and what to do about it, occupies more time of city staff than any other item. But financially the city does well. Since 1959, when they completed purchase of the railroad property and made the parking lots, the gross from the business has totalled over two million dollars.

25 In April 1960 Sausalito felt the sting of one of
the first protest rallies against a state law and
the establishment ever held in California. Such protest rallies have become as common as causes since
then, but the historic first in Sausalito shook the
town and made world wide vibrations. The meeting
was organized to protest the execution of Caryl
Chessman, who had served twelve years on death
row in San Quentin on conviction of rape and
kidnapping. The protest was started accidentally one
evening by George Draper, a newspaper reporter
who had a strong feeling for life (everyone's), and
felt frustrated that he wasn't doing anything about
Chessman's. He wondered how many people felt the
same. Being a good reporter interested in opinions,
he turned to the woman sitting next to him on the
commute bus from San Francisco and mentioned
the Chessman case. She immediately responded that
she felt capital punishment was wrong. "It's com-
pounding a bad deed," responded Penelope Stockley. From this meeting the rally was organized.
Draper and Stockley rented the Gate Theatre on
Bridgeway, arranged for speakers, and with very
little advance publicity the theatre was filled. The

question was answered: many people were concerned about capital punishment and wanted to do something about it. The press and T.V. cameramen covered the rally thoroughly.

During the meeting a plan was evolved to start a flame of life on the top-most hill of Sausalito and to keep the flame alive until the governor either granted a stay of execution or Chessman was killed. A property owner present gave permission for the use of his land. The purpose of the flame was to draw attention to capital punishment and to influence Governor Brown's decision on Chessman. Sally Stanford was present and offered her support both in money and spirit, to help get a butane tank and other equipment. A committee was formed. Volunteers agreed to tend the flame around the clock. Within forty-eight hours all was in readiness.

Just before the meeting ended, Draper announced from the stage that the flame of life was an excellent plan to draw attention to the struggle against the barbarism of a life for a life, "and to start the fire going," he said, "we have arranged for a further demonstration on the sandspit. I urge you all to follow me over there as soon as this meeting closes."

Everyone did, T.V. cameramen and press included. Over five hundred people marched the short distance away and quickly learned that if Draper felt strongly about a flame of life, he had deeper convictions about a conflagration. He had gathered enough wooden and cardboard boxes to make a pile thirty feet high and twenty feet wide. The idea, of course, was to set fire to the boxes and draw attention to their cause. The police had seen the crowd gathering on the sandspit and realized it was not a routine happening. They ordered that no fire be set and gave themselves the difficult task of trying to guard the perimeter of the pile in total darkness. Matches were lighted and thrown at the boxes from various angles. A small flame was started. As one policeman attempted to extinguish the fire, the other one ordered that no one must leave the area until the police found who had thrown the match. It was a foolish order. People were walking away in disgust because the whole pile was not going to go up in flames. One man was handcuffed when he defied the order to remain. The cameras recorded the scene which was shown the next day on news programs. It was the kind of publicity Draper wanted. The huge fire never came off, but it took the entire emergency police force to stop it, plus help from the sheriff's department.

Two nights later the weather was cold, windy, foggy and damp, but more than one hundred people gathered on the hilltop near Wolfback Ridge for ceremonies to start the flame of life. Numerous press representatives, including *Life* magazine, were present. *Life* published a picture of the event in the next issue. The flame was started and guarded constantly by volunteers who had protection from the weather in a house trailer donated to the cause.

For three weeks the flame burned in vigor as Chessman's life ebbed. A continuous protest vigil was held at San Quentin prison gate. Numerous sympathizers assembled, including Marlon Brando, all in a common cause, hoping to draw civilized peoples' attention to a barbaric practice. Perhaps the effort helped for the future, but lessons come hard for the now. On May 2, 1960 Chessman's life was taken. Revenge.

26 　**P**eggy Tolk Watkins was one of Sausalito's most colorful and talented women. There was nothing she couldn't do and very little she hadn't. She was an excellent painter and designer. Her conversation was outstanding, yet she seldom spoke more than five words at a time. She didn't have to. Peggy was a pithy conversationalist whose remarks often cut to the core and exposed the extraneous. She coined words and phrases as fast as a mint. Peggy, for example, was the first to say that psychiatry was nothing but skullduggery. About one of Sausalito's mayors she said: "He's so illiterate he couldn't read an eye chart." Her voice was a little on the kazoo side and seemed to come from inside her gall bladder. Peggy wasn't blessed with good looks. The hard knocks of experience and learning were reflected by the bumps and bruises on her face.

What displeased Peggy more than anything was the plain and ordinary. When it became an irritation she did something about it and always made an improvement. The phrase, "it's good enough!" could set her to learning a whole new art or business to prove that it wasn't good enough. To her "better" was necessary.

One day in 1955 Peggy decided Sausalito needed a restaurant where artists, writers, dreamers, boasters and talkers could gather and feel at ease with each other, swap tales and ideas and be unhurried and welcomed. If anyone else wanted to come in they would be welcomed. So Peggy took possession of a small abandoned building on the waterfront about a hundred yards from the Purity grocery store, and in six weeks she was in business. The building, moved outboard a few feet, is now Scoma's. But it has a history of successfully feeding the populace in a much more informal manner before it became its present operation.

It's a miracle that Peggy was able to open her doors to the public because she was so informal and relaxed about everything. There were laws governing sanitation, fire safety, number of seats for occupancy and other restrictive rules. She tore out a few walls so people could get together, installed a stove and announced she was open for business. It was then she learned that the building inspector would have to look it over, and the county health officer would have to approve of a few things.

"How many seats will you have?" she was asked.

"I hadn't figured on seats, actually. People will find places to sit if they want to," she replied. Her large wide open face, soft brown eyes, announced honesty in clear and distinct terms.

"You must have toilets and wash room," she was told.

"My customers won't expect it," she said.

"There has to be an exit in case of fire."

"There's windows."

"No, that won't do. Are you going to serve wine and beer?"

"I hadn't figured on it. But there'll be a jug. People can help themselves."

There were other details. The kitchen would never do. She was told she would have to have counter space, a refrigerator, hot and cold water, sanitation, sanitation, sanitation. When the inspector finished listing the necessities in the kitchen Peggy remarked she hadn't intended to do any surgery, just cook up a little stew now and then for friends to eat. "It'll be boiled," she reminded the man. "This is not going to be an ordinary restaurant," she said. "It's going to be funky. Know what that means?"

"Not exactly, but I do know what the rules are," he replied.

There were enough violations to discourage an army, but Peggy set about correcting them. With the help of a few inventive Gate 5 people she made changes, and when she called the inspector back he was amazed at what she had done and surprised she would do it. The changes she made were not according to the letter of the law, but he was getting an education in the meaning of funky. Finally he gave his approval, not so much because she had satisfied requirements, but because he figured she wouldn't be in business long anyway.

The Tin Angel opened. It was an instantaneous success. Although it was a little more formal than Peggy liked, still it had her personality. The food was outstanding, but a little restrictive: one item, and that was what she chose to prepare that day. If a customer wanted diversity he had to come often, for she had a different dish each day she was open. If she didn't feel like cooking, she stayed home and painted.

Peggy introduced "camp" decoration to the bay area, and the Tin Angel was the first business house successfully done in this style.

Six months after opening Peggy closed. She was forced to. The inspector returned, and to protect his job he ordered her to comply with all codes. It was too much trouble for Peggy and anyway she didn't care. She had proven she could do it. She sold the business to two young men, who were more serious about running a restaurant, and had the talent to do it. They moved the building out to its present location, made all necessary changes and opened the doors. They changed the name to "Glad Hand." It, too, became a favorite, and soon its reputation grew to the entire bay area. Al and Bob operated the Glad Hand for 20 years, then sold in 1970, but they retained the name for old time's sake. They never used it again.

Peggy went to San Francisco and opened the Fallen Angel, a large entertainment parlor, with drinks and music, in one of the old sporting houses that Sally Stanford operated in her hey-day. Again Peggy's touch dominated; she found talent and gave it an opportunity. It was there that Johnny Mathis got his start.

Peggy Tolk Watkins died in her late fifties after leading several lives. But the ghost of her still walks the streets of Sausalito, her voice haunts with good memories.

In 1957 a few determined citizens of Sausalito stirred up the pot of conservatism enough to make the whole town boil, all in a good cause. It was the first time the high class people on the hill met amicably with the low class flat land residents and later signed their names to the same document. Whatever the motives, the result was a first for Sausalito.

If you walk down Main Street to the Valhalla, there's a wooden walk built over the water that meets another walk at right angles. If you follow that to the end you pass several houses, and on the corner, the old Jack London house. There the wooden path ends where it meets Bridgeway. Actually the walkway is a continuation of Bridgeway, an underwater right of way sixty feet wide that extends along the waterfront to Valley Street. For as long as anyone can remember, the boardwalk has been a favorite walk for residents who meet and talk while watching the tide waters and marine life just a few feet below. As you lean over the rail you have a magnificent view of San Francisco. It never occurred to people as they walked the boards that there was privately owned underwater land between them and San Francisco. But there was. Stretching into the bay were lots one hundred feet deep with another city owned street outboard of them. The realization of private ownership came one day in February 1957 when a man applied for a building permit to erect a huge apartment complex covering all ten lots from Main Street to Richardson. The boardwalk would be torn down and the road right-of-way filled for easy access to the apartments. The cove, as it is called, would be built on. Yes, it was a shame that the view from the houses on the waterfront and the Valhalla would be ruined, but it would also be a shame to prevent the man who owned the property, the right to develop it. The area was zoned for apartments, so he was entitled to build on it. The building permit was issued, for a thirty-six unit apartment complex with floating gardens and yacht facilities.

Mary Lindheim, a potter of exceptional talent, lived in the old Jack London house. Mary wasn't one to accept a ruling as a fait accompli. There was much to be done before construction of the buildings could actually take place and this gave Mary time to think and organize. She started by alerting several people in town and arranged a meeting in her home. There the education started. Within two days everybody in town knew about the proposed apartments. Most were shocked. Only a few said, "If the man owns the property, he should be able to develop it." But Mary, and others

164

like her, were conservationists in the days before the word became so popular. They formed a committee whose aim was simply to prevent the construction. One interested party was Sally Stanford. If the apartments were built in front of her restaurant, she would have more to lose in her terms than the conservationists had to lose in theirs. It's causes such as this that make strange bedfellows. Sally joined the group and paid her attorney to give legal advice in an effort to save the cove. It was a welcome gesture, for the committee was a fledgling in fighting city hall and needed sound guidance. Each meeting drew more people until, in the end, a hall had to be rented. The frequent meetings were necessary to generate interest while stalling so the attorney could come up with strategy. Meanwhile city hall was scoffing at the sophomores on the waterfront who were making loud legal noises but could not be heard beyond their own courtyard.

One cloud in the issue brought out an interesting statement from a councilman. The man who signed the building permit application said he was not the developer and was not at liberty to reveal the developer's name. The committee wanted to know who he was, so he could be approached; perhaps something could be worked out. At a council meeting the chairman of the committee asked if the councilmen knew the developer. None of them did, whereupon one councilman said, "I don't know and don't want to know so I can be impartial in my judgement."

It was a shocking statement.

"That's not logical," replied the chairman, "for it says that you are only impartial to strangers. How about townpeople's applications? Are you prejudiced against them?"

"No. I didn't mean that."

"Perhaps not. But it is what you said."

At long last, the attorney produced the initiative petition. Signatures would be sought to compel a special election at which time voters would decide if the area should be used for recreational purposes. It was a legal handle large enough to be gripped by the committee and the community. Twenty days later a petition bearing over a thousand signatures of qualified voters was presented to City Hall. And just in time, for a barge was in the cove taking borings to determine foundation needs.

The petition upset the councilmen. They had been elected to legislate and dispense justice; they didn't like a group of malcontents telling them what to do. But now they were confronted with legal papers that stated the people had spoken. They had to respond. The staff in city hall could have glanced over the names in twenty minutes to verify the signatures as valid, had they been given the order, but the councilmen stalled and sputtered until they thought of further delay. They asked the city attorney for his opinion. John Ehlen was never one to make a hasty judgement. It took him ten minutes to say he would have to give the matter some heavy thought and research. "Two weeks might be enough," he said, "but I doubt it." A month went by. Then the crucial meeting. Ehlen stated that in his opinion the petitions were not in proper form. The Save The Cove committee was stunned. Now it would become a legal argument between two attorneys, and everyone knew that those discussions take time. In the meantime the barge was working away.

Worse luck. Sally had fired her attorney. The committee was left to its own devices, but not for long. The citizenry was aroused. The petition had asked for the issue to be voted on and, when that was refused them, their democratic rights had been stepped on. This would never do. Some people who signed the petition, but stated they would vote against condemnation, said they should have the right to vote on it. Attorneys by the score came out of the woodwork and offered their counsel. It took a while to reorganize, but the delay turned out best for the committee and the entire town.

The concentration had been entirely on the underwater

lots outboard of the boardwalk. But with a little investigation it was learned that all the land along the length of Bridgeway outboard of the street for one hundred feet, from the Jack London house to Ondine restaurant was privately owned, except for a few lots that had been purchased by the city for back taxes. The most magnificent view in the bay area could be obliterated by a wall of apartments if the owners of the property had chosen to develop their land. This information gave impetus to the Save The Cove committee. If the boardwalk lots were built on, it would be a precedent for the other lands to be developed. Public outcry was unanimous: nothing should be built on that land. But how to prevent it was the problem. The city council had stated that it was opposed to condemnation for recreational needs, because to do that, the owners would have to be compensated, and the city had no money to purchase the property. The philosophy was that the land was privately owned, and the free enterprise system must be protected. It was a complicated affair that finally settled itself by a factor more powerful than the laws: money.

Because public sentiment against the apartments was so strong, the banks were unwilling to loan money to the developer. They felt certain that a way would be found to legally prevent construction. When this was learned, the value of the land dropped and the owner offered it to the city at a good price and terms. In addition, all the privately-owned land along Bridgeway dropped in value. The town was elated. Immediately donations started coming in at a great rate, for now public ownership was within reason. And then the Sausalito Foundation joined the cause.

This organization, founded just a short time before by a group of dedicated citizens who felt privileged to live in Sausalito and wanted to show their appreciation, had as its purpose the perpetuation of everything that made the town a good place to live. And if that wasn't enough, they wished to add to the amenities. They sponsored benefits, sought donations, gave of their own money, time and talents to purchase works of art, buy small pieces of land for mini-parks and playgrounds, purchase library books, provide scholarships for children, and benches for rest and viewing and presented it all to the town. Gestures such as this are commonly called civic pride, but whatever it's called, this was the Foundation's method of expressing gratitude. When it decided to help purchase waterfront property, it took but six weeks until the Foundation had raised $60,000 and had promises for more. The Foundation offered the money to the city, and it was happily accepted. The city made an offer to all the owners of the underwater land, and it was accepted. In a short time the agreements were made and the land purchased.

Untold numbers of tourists have turned off the Golden Gate Bridge to curve their way downhill to Sausalito, thrilled by the view, only to find upon reaching Bridgeway that there was one continuous line of autos inching along at a slow snail's pace. But once on the flat road, with the wide open view of the bay, the sea lion statue, the cool bay breezes, all tempers calm, the traffic could stop and no one would complain. That stretch of Bridgeway is the great leveler, a psyche panacea. Few people realize that without the efforts and civic spirit of Mary Lindheim, that stretch of waterfront road would be a boxed-in fume trap today, with buildings on one side, the hill on the other. Her monument is open space.

This is but one example of plans not completed, buildings not built that were proposed for Sausalito. Those unrealized plans and structures on paper have as much to do with present day Sausalito as the buildings and shops now in operation.

27   **A** few of Sausalito's artists were so good their products were in demand all over the United States. One such artist was Dave Morris, a potter. Dave had so many orders from leading San Francisco stores that he would have had to mass-produce to satisfy their demands. Dave would never do that. He had too much integrity to turn out something just for money; he was an artist whose pots were so good his throw-aways were grabbed up by friends who felt privileged to get them. Dave and his wife Helen worked together at a slow exact pace in their studio home on the waterfront just a half-mile north of the main business section of town. This was the La Paz pottery. As the tide waters slapped beneath the floor of their one-room living area and shop, they shaped their pots, mixed the glazes and prepared for the monthly firing. Besides unusual and utilitarian shapes, Dave experimented with glazes never used in the pottery business and perfected some that are the envy of potters throughout the world.

After the day's work, Helen prepared food on a stove Dave had made from iron bars suspended above gas burners salvaged from old water heaters. It was an excellent stove that allowed the bars to roll, overcoming the friction of a heavy pan on a hard surface. As Helen cooked, Dave relaxed with his guitar, playing and singing mostly Mexican music. Helen frequently joined in. Before the evening ended several friends had arrived, bringing wine, another guitar or two.

The La Paz pottery was separated by a thin wall of plywood from a ship repair shop. One night in 1960 a fire started in the paint locker and in minutes cans of paint and turpentine exploded in a fury of flames. The plywood ignited and burned with intense heat. Helen and Dave each grabbed a guitar and escaped. That's all they saved. The building was a total loss. La Paz pottery was out of business, the kiln destroyed, pipes and gauges melted to a glob. Heavy timbers fell and smashed the brick to pieces. Dave and Helen and their son, Nick, moved in with friends.

The owners of Ondine restaurant held a benefit party for the burned out family. Artists contributed their works, Ondine the food, entertainers from San Francisco night clubs their talent, for a spectacular show. Invitations were sent out and publicity gained through newspapers. It was a tremendous success in cooperation, generosity, charity, humanity and just as important, it was a success financially. The money was turned over to Dave and Helen, and they prudently used it to build a home and studio a few miles from Sausalito. There they continue to contribute great art forms to the world.

To list all other good artists living in Sausalito in the '50s would fill a small book. Two outstanding ones were Keith Monroe and Walter Kuhlman. In 1957 they received the fame and international recognition which they deserved. Both won the Graham Fellowship award. Kuhlman was selected for his painting and Monroe for sculpture. The ten thousand dollar award was given to the two artists for their outstanding ability and consistent progress of several years standing. Monroe was a pioneer in steel sculpture. The recognition was important to the artists, but the money was more useful. Monroe used his money to go to Spain where he could live and study under other innovative sculptors who were well known at the time. Kuhlman was a cool and serious man, thankful for the award and fame, but he looked upon the money as a means to take some financial pressure off his mind. He had a family to support, and had been helping the budget by washing dishes in the Glad Hand restaurant, a task he didn't mind because he could think art while earning money. Kuhlman's reaction to word that he had received the Graham award tells something of the type of man he was. At two o'clock in the morning a reporter friend working the night shift of the *San Francisco Chronicle* saw an AP report telling of the awards. He immediately phoned Kuhlman, woke him from his peaceful sleep and told him the news. The artist was a little cool about it, but thanked his friend and as he got back to bed his wife asked who in God's name would phone at that hour of the night.

"It was Tom at the Chronicle," he said.

"What in hell did he want?"

"He said I won ten thousand bucks and the Graham award."

Nora leaped out of bed. "Walt, Oh my God. That's wonderful. Wow! Think of it. Really? I can't believe it. Aren't you happy?"

"Sure I am," replied Walt, crawling under the covers, "it's great. But the bastard could have waited until morning to tell me."

Most citizens of Sausalito were surprised to learn of the popularity of their town. Living there was far different from merely visiting. For some people the change was hard to understand. The number of gift shops perplexed them. But worse, with each gift shop, a resident-serving shop went out.

The Kettle was one instance. Situated alongside the popular Bob's Market, on Bridgeway, the Kettle delicatessen replaced a tailor. The tailor was ready to retire and happy to sell out, but the citizens expected him to stay forever, sewing and mending to their needs. They wouldn't patronize a delicatessen. The theory of the owner was that because so many couples living in Sausalito worked all day in San Francisco,

171

they would enjoy the opportunity to stop by on their way home and purchase a casserole and other ready-made delights for their dinner. It should have worked. The establishment was first class, but did very little business. Bob and Ben made good thick sandwiches and served wholesome food, but not often enough. Citizens quickly learned that the end of the week was the best time to patronize the shop, because they were served larger portions. The owners had a policy of starting out with everything fresh on Monday, and not wanting to throw away food they gave it away. It was good philosophy, but poor business.

Leo Krikorian had his eye on the shop. Leo was getting tired of the beatnik generation on Upper Grant Avenue in San Francisco, where he successfully operated the Coexistence Bagel shop for years. When he bought the Kettle, he cut out the hot casseroles and many of the fancy prepared foods, installed more tables and chairs, and concentrated on serving quick sandwiches and salads to tourists. To make the Kettle more of a tourist attraction, he commissioned Bill Dempster to paint murals on the walls depicting well known Sausalito residents. Dempster was an outstanding artist, who at that time in his career, specialized in caricatures and had several cartoons in national publications. With a few judicious strokes, Dempster could capture the subject's spirit as well as his features. For months he worked on the murals before finishing the two walls. The results were a work of art, expertly executed and showing great imagination. Gloss is shown snapping tickets to windshields, Mr. Loudon behind the counter, Courtland Mudge serving beer at the Old Town Coffee House, and a host of other well-knowns, forty in all. It was well received by almost everyone in town. The only criticisms came from people who wished they had been depicted but weren't. If one looks closely at the upper right hand corner, he'll see the artist being chased out of town by a group of angry citizens.

172

28　That bronze sculptured sea lion sitting proud and defiant off shore at Hearst point, was put permanently in place in 1966. But it has a history of several years before that, when its counterpart existed in concrete and haydite. Viewers from all over the world have pleased their eyes and senses with the work, and some have written letters of appreciation to the city for providing the outstanding statue. The truth of the matter is that the city contributed only $100.00 toward the permanent sculpture, and dragged its feet doing that.

Sausalito has always had a reputation for its art. One would think it is an annex to the Louvre. But the reputation is not due to city policy. About the only credit the town can take is that it allows artists to live there. It does nothing to encourage them though, and sometimes the toleration gets sticky. What works of art the city displays now and then have all been contributed. The city has never had an art commission, never participated in art functions except to grant a use permit annually for an art festival, never contributed money to further art. It has no public gallery, therefore never purchased any works. There are no studios that the city helped finance, no scholarships. The city fathers are proud of the reputation for art and have traded on it; the result shows up in sales tax dollars left by tourists. Peggy Tolk Watkins, in one of her less charitable moods said, "It's better the city doesn't try to do anything. Like the waters of Marienbad, what could they do to improve it?"

Al Sybrian is the sculptor responsible for the Sea Lion. Al was well known in Sausalito for his drawings, stone walls, drinking and conversation. He was good in all, and oftentimes excelled in the latter two. He could drop in to say hello of an afternoon and make his goodbyes five days later. When he left he usually went right back to a wall he was building and stayed on the job 16 hours a day for a week, sort of like repentance. It wasn't that he felt an obligation to his employer, but Al was an artist, and after several days of non-creation he was uneasy with himself. The walls he built were works of art. Al lived in a small house directly beneath the old Hearst wall, which is half way between Ondine Restaurant and the Valhalla. Dr. and Mrs. Wiper owned the house where Hearst wanted to build. Sybrian did small jobs in exchange for rent. From his house he could see sea lions on the rocks not over a hundred feet away. He sketched them endlessly. One day in 1957 he talked to a neighbor, Mr. Gratama, and said he would like to make a sculpture of a sea lion to be placed on the waterfront, but he had no money for materials.

"How much will it take?"

"I don't know. Maybe a hundred dollars."

Mr. Gratama talked to Julie Sweet, another neighbor, and the Wipers. Together they put up the money. Al set to work immediately. The half finished wall he was working on would have to wait. When Al was inspired his concentration never wavered. Within three months he had finished. He notified his benefactors and they came to see what he had done. They were amazed. Instantly they recognized it as being a good work of art. They all knew of Al's ability, but now they were looking at an accomplishment that just a short time before was only a promise. The sculpture stood four feet high, molded in concrete with the slight pink color from haydite. The lines were graceful, yet pronounced, and the turn of the head was a position familiar to everyone who has ever watched sea lions. The party exclaimed profusely, and like thousands since, could not keep their hands off of it. It had that appeal.

The statue sat around for a few months while Al and his benefactors wondered what to do with it, where best to display it. The most obvious spot was overlooked for a long time until Steese happened by.

"Public land, on the waterfront," he said. "Right outside your door. On top of that old manhole cover down there. It gets covered up during high tides, so we can get it out there during a low one. Perfect place. When do you want to do it?"

"During the next low tide," said Al.

A phone call or two got enough friends to carry the sea lion down the rocky beach and put her in place. It was 1 a.m. when they accomplished the task. The next morning a traffic jam occurred on Bridgeway as commuters stopped to view the new occupant of the waterfront.

For eight years she sat there unperturbed, indomitable, giving joy and satisfaction to viewers. Her grace and silence became a trademark. Homeward bound weary commuters got a lift when viewing her, children played on her back, thousands of pictures were taken of her by tourists and townspeople. She was growing as popular as Denmark's Little Mermaid. But the sea lion wasn't made of good material. High tides, winds, battering logs and debris during winter storms had been beating against her unprotected sides, taking their toll. The sea lion was breaking up. Cracks in the concrete grew larger, pieces were falling off.

175

Al looked the sculpture over one day and announced he was going to destroy it. As the creator he had the right to do it, and his heart told him he must.

Enid Foster, the grand dame of Sausalito artists, heard about it and knowing Al, she knew he would do it. She immediately wrote the city council asking for funds to cast the statue in bronze. An outcry from many residents was heard, so the council, in their charitable wisdom, agreed to contribute $100 and made a plea that the citizens get behind the effort to make it a community project. The job would cost $3,000, of which the artist would get $700. That was a fair price, for there was much work to do. Al would have to make a mold from what was left of the statue.

Weeks went by. A few contributions trickled in, mainly from artists. Sybrian had moved the original sculpture to San Francisco in the expectation that funds would come in. He was getting discouraged. Then the Sausalito Foundation put up the money and the project was completed.

So in 1966 a bronze sea lion was placed in her present position.

Al Sybrian wasn't present on the day of official dedication. He was in San Francisco helping Steese install a new vat for Steam Beer. A more important mission.

29 The annual art festival held in Sausalito is a sudsy and weak spinoff from the original. And like everything else in Sausalito it has become crowded, commercial and distorted. One reason for the change is that there's no room for the likes of the festivals in the past. The originals were held on the Sandspit years before the Spinnaker was built, where there was room to spread out. Without the asphalt parking lots, the Bank of America building and the restaurant, there was nothing but open space from Bridgeway to Belvedere. A proper sized piece of land for a celebration.

The old festivals needed a wide expanse because things were done in a grand manner. They were more than an art show, they were pageants and extravaganzas. There was great festivity, with dancing at night, live music that entertained, not

177

distracted, first-rate original dramas, pleasure, gayety and celebrations. Something for everyone. No one ever left those festivals disappointed. There was plenty of room for an artist to arrange and display his work properly. Each participant had a small gallery where viewers could step in and study, and not be distracted out of the corner of his eye by a bright color next door. The individual artists made their own display stands. "You take that corner over there," or "How about that section?" they were told. A pattern of sorts, but no conformity. There weren't as many viewers in those days, but there were more serious art lovers. It's all a numbers game now, the success of an art festival is measured by attendance.

One holdover the present festivals maintain is the three-day duration, but for a different purpose. It was necessary in 1954 to be open three days because it took nearly that long to properly see every exhibit. The pace was slow and easy with places to sit and talk with the artist, to get to know him or her. And because one purpose of the affair was to have an enjoyable time, there was not the haste to get through and away for a breath of fresh air. After looking at a display for half an hour or so, you might sit down and have a cup of coffee, then say to your party, "Let's go over and look at that one for a while." And so it went.

Varda, George Hitchcock, Ben Irvin, Ed Spolin and others were the designers and builders of the first art festivals. It was Varda's influence that was mainly responsible, and Varda never did anything in half measures. Huge banners of gay, distinct and compatible colors seventy-five feet high were erected all around the area, announcing a festival was taking place. A stage four feet high was erected for the dramas. A large concrete platform was poured for dancing. There was continuous entertainment, music, puppets, mimes, jugglers, magicians, and of course, art in action: huge potter's wheels, craftsmen, cartoonists. Fireworks at night from a barge out in the water. At four o'clock each afternoon a large boat would

178

be seen approaching from down the bay. Activity stopped while people watched its progress. This was the signal that the drama would soon be presented, for the boat carried the actors. It was gaily decorated for the occasion, with bright sails and flying banners. As it approached the crowds lined the shore. The actors disembarked and marched single file through a path lined with people. The actors, in costume, faces heavily disguised with makeup and masks, were unrecognizable.

These daily theatricals were the highlight of the festival. Written by Hitchcock or DiSuvero, and being a masque or tableau, there was great emphasis on colorful stage setting, costumes and disguises. Oftentimes written in Shakespearean verse, they were clever, bawdy, and always comical. A great deal of talent and creative energy went into those plays. The only reward was a good time doing it and the satisfaction of having brought pleasure to the audience.

Aside from the joyous spirit of the occasion, the art was of a more serious nature than the present festivals. No dabblers or weekend hobbyists were allowed. The artists were hand-picked by a panel of experts and then invited to participate. It was an honor to have been chosen. And because the calibre of the artists and their reputation was well known, there were always serious art collectors and gallery owners in the audience.

A series of circumstances caused the big change in the art festivals. After the Spinnaker restaurant was built, the entire sandspit became privately developed and closely guarded. Then the bank was built and the parking lots were blacked over to start the green rolling. Varda and others didn't want to make a career of building art festivals. They had proved they could do it, and had their enjoyment. Now to move on to something else. For a few years there were no festivals. Then a few young and serious artists became enthusiastic. Spearheaded by Bill Kirsch, who designed the projects with banners by Sonja Pimentel, two commendable shows were held in the parking lot next to the bank. These were good festivals. But they caused the biggest traffic jams in the entire history of Sausalito. The merchants complained of the lack of business. People came to town by the tens of thousands, but they didn't shop. That would never do. The shop-owners marched on city hall. They showed statistics: the loss of sales tax dollars to the city treasury. Arguments were made about traffic, fire and police safety and the lack of public facilities. The merchants were bothered about continual requests for the use of toilets. All weak arguments to be sure. The festival paid for private police to direct traffic, for off-duty firemen to man a truck downtown, and there were portable toilets, albeit not enough. But the city council ruled out any more festivals in the business district. The merchants as usual displayed their philosophy of immediate greed and ungratefulness. For years they had been trading on Sausalito's reputation as an artists' town, selling goods to tourists attracted to the town to see for themselves this great art center. For three days out of the year the reputation could be maintained. The merchants could coast on the money brought in during all other days, but they wanted every single day possible.

30 One day in 1960 Ernie hung a sign on the Port Hole door reading "SALE." The residents were shocked. Ernie had never had a sale, and had never bargained with anyone. He wouldn't, so they couldn't. The sign was more than an announcement of goods to be sold, it was a grave message, an irreversible declaration. The Port Hole was going out of business. It had lost the battle to tourism. After all the questions were asked the answer was simple, "people and demand." The owner of the building was offered $500 per month rent. Ernie was paying $100 and couldn't go more than $150. His business was resident-serving. The tourists who wandered in

181

walked around a little, then out, remarking how quaint the shop was. Ernie couldn't live on adjectives. Tourists didn't buy his goods, they were looking for something shiny, new and useless. If they returned in a few months they'd find it. A gift shop was going in. "What? Another one?" asked the residents. "Good Lord, that's the last thing we need. What about the cleaning and mending? Where will we get that done?" Service shops may be necessary to a town, but no law says that a landlord has to take less rent just to please the people.

So Ernie retired and went to Lake County, which he deserved, and Sausalito got another garish shop it didn't need. Nothing for residents, but tourists could buy anything from alfalfa tea to zodiac charts.

While Ernie's life in Lake County was changing to a more placid one, Brooks, the butcher, was going in the opposite direction, from placidity to activity. As the meat sales to residents dropped off, Brooks started making cold-cut sandwiches for tourists. Next came coffee. In a few months he was in the take-out food business and concentrating less on knighted steaks for residents. Brooks made good sandwiches, but his nature as a butcher was against him at first. Thick cuts of meat to retain juices and flavor were all right for steaks and roasts, but it would never do for sandwiches. Using his steel honed, long bladed knife he soon found that the thinner the slices the more tender the meat. He quickly learned how to build up a thick sandwich that was both appealing and nutritious. Later he got a machine that cut thin slices from roasts that his wife baked in her home. Now the yield was doubled. In a few months he quit retailing messy fresh provender at 99 cents per pound and sold roast beef at $27 per pound. Out went the high display counter, the walk-in refrigerator, the Brooks personality. In came a low counter, stools, grills, huge coffee urns, waitresses, cooks, dishwashers and worries. He now had a restaurant and new troubles. Brooks served the best short-order food in town, but not without a price: his own. He became a hurried businessman trying to keep an eye on all phases of the business at one time, while simultaneously frying steak and eggs and hash browns for a customer. And then there was the help. It was hard to get good workers. They'd stay a while, then leave. Endless. If he wasn't cooking or adjusting the slicing machine, he was sitting at the end stool, a coffee cup to his lips, elbows on the formica, eyes darting back and forth. His wife worked by his side. Their business was brisk, but it took constant attention. Brooks had long ago lost his, "hello, how are you?" greeting. Most of his customers were tourists. He recognized their money but didn't know their names.

For every gift shop that came in some nostalgia went out. When an art gallery opened in 1962 it was a surprise to residents. An art gallery wasn't needed in Sausalito. Any time residents wanted to buy a painting or sculpture they went to an artist's studio. But the merchant had other ideas. The most important was to not sell local artists' work. He couldn't and stay in business. He didn't intend to sell to residents, and he knew that tourists on a trip buy gay, bright and useless souvenirs. He would trade on Sausalito's reputation as an artist's town and offer the tourists a painting they could afford. So the merchant filled the shop with imitation canvases depicting mechanical sunsets, desert scenes, babbling blue brooks, blossoming trees, sunlit mountains against blue skies, a dirt road overhung with thick tree branches and an occasional horse or puppy for a bit of life. All painting came from Southern California, all blues from the same tube, and the frames were instant antique; a bent nail laid sideways and struck leaving a dent simulating termite-eaten holes; indigestion. He sold thousands of pictures and ordered more by their numbers; send fifty number six or twenty number eight. But most tourists believed they had an original painting from Sausalito, the art capital of the west.

Other changes were happening, some major, some minor, but all significant. All contributed to the demise of a diminishing little town. The municipal dock where some residents tied their boats, did their weekly shopping, met friends and sailed home was towed away, abandoned. Too many outsiders were using it. The council was warned of liability. "But this is a waterfront town. There must be a public dock," argued sailing enthusiasts. But the council decided the risk was too great. A steady, progressive, irreversible amputation was occurring in Sausalito. And with each physical loss, there was a spiritual decline.

The councilmen were powerless to do anything about the growing tourism. There has to be commercial zoning, and shops are permitted in that zone. The nature of the shop cannot be dictated. Even if the council wanted to change the ordinance and not allow gift shops downtown, it couldn't define gifts as opposed to utility. A bar of soap could be a gift. Nor could the council limit the number of shops unless it could prove that more would be against the health, safety and welfare of the community. It would be very difficult to prove that selling Japanese fans is against a town's welfare. But they did act against take-out food stores. In 1968 they decided they'd better, or be drowned in garbage. There were seven such stores at the time and the amount of waste thrown on the streets and sidewalks was evidence enough to prove a case against the people's health. An ordinance was passed preventing more take-out food stores to open, but existing ones could remain.

Sausalito was changing so fast it was difficult to keep up with it. In a week's time there could be and often were three new shops. They crowded into places that citizens didn't know existed. Most were partitioned off from a larger store. The town was doing business so fast it didn't know how to handle it. It should have been protecting its character, but it was too busy taking on a new one. Within a few years the reputation changed from a quiet, quaint little town to "you've gotta go there and see the shops, they're so cute and far out. And the people you see. Why there's nothing like it."

It was true. The boutique shops were a maze of "things" and a miracle of imagination. Residents scoffed, but tourists bought. The streets and sidewalks were crowded with jaywalking visitors holding up traffic, window shopping, licking on candied apples, or ice cream cones, or digging into fish and chips or hot tacos, finishing with a napkin swipe across the mouth before dropping the paper on the sidewalk. Downtown was also a place to be seen and display an unusual dress or an eye-catching undress. Men, in various costumes, exhibited anatomy which told more about the character of the man that what he wore. It was a constant parade of faces, forms and fashions. An unbelievable show that drew outsiders just to sit and watch.

There were a few diehard residents who thought of the tourists as visitors to a carnival who would leave when the show was over and things would get back to normal. Optimists. Mr. Loudon in the hardware store was one. He continued serving residents, trying to ignore tourists. Each morning he put the hobby horse out on the sidewalk, but fewer and fewer Sausalito children were using it. The mothers weren't coming downtown so often. Frequently, too, Mr. Loudon would have to ask a grown man to get off the horse. A celebrating tourist.

Big Bart was called into the police station one day where the chief told him he could no longer sell his carvings on the street.

"But I make my living doing that. How come?" he asked.

"They call it discrimination," replied the chief. "If I let you do it, I have to let all peddlers. We've been getting too many complaints lately."

"About me?"

"No. About those young men selling newspapers. We

had to clamp down on them. There's a law against peddling on the sidewalks."

Suddenly, it seemed, three young men started hawking newspapers around the business district. They walked up and down, rude and aggressive, shoving the rag into pedestrians faces, coercing, accosting and nuisancing up the business section. The papers, printed underground in Berkeley and The Haight-Ashbury, were perhaps popular amongst troglodytes in those areas, but Kansas plainsmen and Vermont visitors weren't interested. Complaints were heard at city hall. When enough piled up, the police had to invoke the ordinance. And this meant Bart would have to stop also.

The little triangle park across the street from Jan's became a stage for exhibitionists. The audience was huge, the price was right. "You can see anything in Sausalito," was a familiar phrase. All types of dress and undress to please both the curious and the exhibitors. The latter came from San Francisco mostly. Daring, harmless kids who found the Haight-Ashbury acid scene too extreme for their protests and adventures. They met every day in the park and on the sidewalk adjoining. To the delight of the audience, they tried to outdo each other with displays of nudity, crudity and amateur eroticism, often more pitiful than entertaining. The young girls, tender and beautiful, lying on the grass, exposing their thighs and undeveloped torsos were like flowers, not ready for pollination, good to look at but lacking the maturity to blossom. While guitars strummed unrecognizable tunes and drums beat arrythmically in constant monotony, braless, pantless girls allowed the boys' hands to play tunes over their flesh beneath tent-like garments. It was an act, poorly done, but it served the purpose. They were making their anti-adult statements. They weren't speaking very loud, but it was plainly said. People watched or there would have been no show. In the audience were a few latent voyeurs who enjoyed their thrills until they couldn't stand the ache in their groins, then walked

186

away gingerly and said, disgustedly, "Those kids are simply awful. They'll do anything." While they were standing there watching, they didn't know where their own children were or what they were doing. But they were wrong about their opinion of the exhibitionists. Those kids weren't interested in sex orgies. If they were they would have been on a waterbed where they could demonstrate their durability and acrobatic skill. What went on in the park was nothing more than mild, tactile finger dancing no more thrilling to watch than a melting iceberg.

The little park was impossible to use for rest and gossip, eating a lunch or sunning a child. There was constant noise, beer drinking, pestering, obscenities and general abuse of adult citizens. The council couldn't make a discriminatory ordinance that would prohibit some age groups from using the park. Because older citizens never drank beer in the park, a law was considered making that illegal. Despite protests from younger citizens, the law was passed. But in six weeks the council was considering closing the park altogether. It would be one way to dispel all the complaints, get rid of the young people hanging around town panhandling, insulting and giving the town a bad reputation.

(Some of the panhandlers were poets. One time your author was stopped. "Brother," said the young man, "I'm just a small coin away from reality. Could you help me?" I thought a moment. "What would it take to reach satori?" I asked. A pause. His bright mind was working. "I've been there. Now I want to return to reality.")

But mainly the park department reported that the gardens were costing four times as much to keep in repair because of the foot traffic. The grass couldn't be reseeded fast enough to keep up with the destruction. Mr. Thompson had quit growing flowers. The beds were ignored, tramped and packed into dirt paths. Roses never blossomed on the hedge. If a little bud showed up it was snitched before it developed. So the park was closed to the public. KEEP OUT! Fences were installed where roses once grew. The residents hadn't abused the park, but public means everyone. Mothers, children and merchants were prohibited. This was a serious loss to Sausalito. A price that had to be paid.

In 1963 Jack Aranson opened the theatre next door to the hardware store and treated Sausalito to first class live entertainment. The treat wasn't intentional. Aranson had expected more than adding to his experience. Aranson and his wife Mary Rose McMaster were veterans of the theatre and every production they staged was first class. For two years they struggled while sparse audiences enjoyed their efforts.

Some merchants did what they could to encourage Aranson's group. In back of the theatre was a courtyard, extending behind several business houses. Very little of the area was used except for the hardware store. Aranson needed dressing rooms. The 7-Seas bar offered rest rooms for the purpose. Holes were cut in fences and a path was made. The Fire Chief demanded a place for audiences to escape in an emergency. Mr. Loudon allowed Aranson to open the fence and let people spill into his backyard if they needed to. It was a kind offer, but opening the fence exposed an unbelievable barricade of hardware entanglements. With sweat and ingenuity Aranson made an opening that satisfied the chief.

After two years Aranson had to give up. Culture and commerce didn't mix. Tourists now stride about in the old theatre, emitting expletives over creative merchandise where thespians once strode about emoting and creating memorable moments.

31 The inevitable happened. In 1963 the Purity grocery store closed its doors. Not even a sale. No warning. Open one day, doors barred the next. All goods moved to a new and shiny location in Mill Valley. Scotty, Dotty, the friendly butchers who knew individual preferences, gone. And so was the cold refrigerated drinking fountain, the familiar squeaky board immediately inside the front door, sawdust, the chance meetings with friends and neighbors. Statistics, figures, that was the story. There simply wasn't enough business, and it didn't take genius to see it wouldn't improve. Tourists didn't buy groceries and it was too much trouble in the stop-and-go traffic for residents to go to the market. If they did, the annoyance was aggravated when they attempted to drive out into the constant line of autos parading into town with bumpers so close there was no room for consideration. Horns did little good for they were heard from all angles all day long.

Bob's Market closed a few weeks later. It was as if the two grocery stores were having a contest of endurance. In this case the one who hung on the longest lost the most. Bob's had a sale, diminishing prices as stock diminished. A gamble to buyers. So now Sausalito was left with two small grocery stores on either edge of town. The closest supermarket was in Mill Valley.

Perhaps the worst blow to the residents came in 1964 with Ray's announcement that he would have to close the shoe repair shop. His lease had run out and the owner of the building had many high offers. He chose one who paid $550 a month, with a ten-year lease and an escalating clause making rent $900 a month for the last three years. It was a typical price to pay for shop space in Sausalito. Ray had been paying $150 and having a hard time meeting that. Residents were stunned. "Oh, no," they said. It was spoken with sincere sorrow, as if a dear friend who had worked hard and long to achieve recognition in his field was struck with a fatal disease. A catastrophe, an unbelievable injustice. His shop was an institution in town; an old friend who was always there when you needed him. And now he was leaving. Crowded out by commercialism. After the initial blow passed, many residents got together to discuss it. A committee was formed. A resolution would be submitted to the city council requesting the council to refuse a business license to the Afro-Asian gift shop which was going in. "It's time we speak up and let the council know how we feel," said the committee. "Maybe we can save this town yet." They were dead serious and believed their request would be granted.

When the matter was brought up at a council meeting,

the chambers were filled with residents, many of whom had never been to a council meeting. They got instant education.

An hour and a half discussion ensued before the subject was finished, dismissed. No resolution or motion was made. There was no vote. Yet it was all perfectly democratic. The councilmen patiently listened to every argument, asked some questions, allowed everyone to speak who wished to, and appeared to be carefully weighing all arguments before making up their minds. Because no one opposed the citizens' request, those present were heartened and certain the resolution would be adopted. Ray would be able to stay. But after everyone had been heard, the city attorney was asked for his opinion on the legality of the request. He explained that it would be illegal. City ordinances allow shops in the commercial district, the area is zoned for them. Denying this application would be discriminatory.

"But we don't need another gift shop," shouted Art Biggs.

"That may be true," replied the attorney. "Then it must be shown that this one is against the health, safety and welfare of the community." He spoke in such a low, calm, avuncular voice it wouldn't have been surprising to see him hand out candy.

This took the councilmen off the hook. But they knew from the beginning that such a resolution was illegal. A week before the meeting they had a file from the attorney explaining in detail the illegality and what his opinion would be at the meeting. They could have avoided the hour and a half discussion by explaining the legal opinion at the start, but it wouldn't have looked democratic if they had.

The sympathy of most of the councilmen was for Ray and the resolution, but they couldn't ignore the attorney's advice. He thought that if they denied the use permit for a gift shop and the applicant took the city to court they were sure to lose the case, which would cost the city much money.

191

During the last few weeks of Ray's lease, there was a steady parade of residents coming and going from his shop. They came to express their sorrow. Some offered the basement of their homes for temporary location. Real estate agents attempted to find a new location, but none was available. A visit to the shop was a sad experience. Huge motors were being dismantled, the guts of the dying patient being removed bit by bit, until the shop was a shell with no soul. Some of the suffering was alleviated temporarily by the numerous bottles given to Ray, and toasts drunk to him, his future, his past, his service to the community. An artist painted one window of the shop depicting well known characters around town, all going toward Ray's, showing Ray, the king, the leader, in a typical pose, apron, shoe, hammer, smile, concern. Ray's final act was to turn over 75 pairs of unclaimed and repaired shoes to the Salvage Shop. Some were bought for souvenirs. As Varda said, "A pity. His last didn't last."

As the persistent tentacles of commercialism consumed the resident-serving shops, it was like the jungle where the strongest vegetation entwines and captures the weak. The souvenir boutiques and artsy-crafty shops, fed by rich tourists, multiplied and grew stronger. Soon they would capture all the ground left. There wasn't much. A hardware store, a bank or two, two drugstores and Jan's. Then suddenly Jan's went so fast the coffee never got cold. The insides were gutted, the exterior "cleaned up," as they say, which means façaded with resawn redwood plywood and heavy molding. Then the doors were opened to a thick beefeaters red carpet, wall-to-wall and a quarter of the way to the ceiling. A man's clothing shop. Pardon. A boutique. Not an emporium where one could purchase a pair of work socks and heavy Levis, nor a simple business suit. This exclusive shop catered to unusual men wanting to look unusual. Tight torso fitting trousers to display anatomy, bright and colorful to attract the eye. A costume of sorts, an announcement.

192

Although sympathy was high for the loss of Jan's, as it had been for Ray's, no attempt was made to save her shop. Residents would miss the coffees, conversation, conviviality, but they were getting hardened to the losses of favorite places. For months the counter had been lined with unfamiliar faces and the park across the street no longer allowed mothers and children on the grounds. Bart and his bathing show had long passed, and it was not relaxing to sit and talk while worrying about the parking meter. It was a shame, that's all, a shame. The rate at which parking meters were being installed on Sausalito streets, one would think that the city's mantra was meters meters meters meters.

Mrs. Goodale closed the Sea Spray Inn one month after parking meters were installed on Bridgeway in front of her restaurant. The meters weren't the only reason, but their presence tipped the scale. After twenty two years of spending eighteen hours a day on her feet, her legs started giving trouble. She bore the pain for nearly a year, then gave up. Many offers were made for the restaurant, but she never considered one. The equipment was moved out, the sign taken down, and the large room re-converted to her living room. It was 1955 when she mixed her last gravy, satisfied her last customer. For seven years after that Mrs. Goodale enjoyed the feeling of a job well done as she lounged in her living room and watched old customers walk by on the sidewalk.

Sausalito also lost the excellent and always exciting Little Theatre group. Since 1954 that group of stage enthusiasts had performed steadily, eager to give their community top entertainment. The excellence of their performances brought many patrons from San Francisco. All the participants lived in Sausalito, actors, actresses and backstage helpers; a community effort of joy and pride. The theatre was in a large room back of the Plaza bar, and was only accessible by going through the bar. The owner donated the use of the room, but he made out all right by pre, during and after performance sales. There was nothing unique about the group. All small towns have them; stage struck thespians eager to prove their talent and willing to work and cooperate to do it. But one day a clever visionary saw the possibility of several shops, (the magic word in Sausalito), in place of the theatre room. An inventive architect transformed the bar and the room to create an arcade with several cubicles put together like a puzzle to make the maximum number. It was all done with city approval; shops for tourists, nothing for residents.

A few leaders of the theatre group sat silently and dejectedly in the back of the meeting room listening to the developer's arguments in favor of the shops. 'Sales taxes, parking fees, revenue, city treasury.' There are no stronger words. One citizen was moved to suggest that the city buy the building and support the theatre to help hold the town together and continue the tradition and encourage community participation. One councilman said he sympathized with the sentiments, but that a theatre in the middle of the commercial area didn't make much sense. "There's other buildings in town where the theatre group can continue their good work. And if I know those people they'll find one."

They were determined people, but he knew and everyone else knew that there was no other building. A little effort was spent trying to locate one, but soon the spirit died. Another vital resident serving use was abolished quickly, decisively. A common pattern in Sausalito.

Late in 1964, Mr. Loudon received a letter from the owner of the building that his lease would not be renewed. He had six months to clear out of the building. Six months to clear out thirty-eight years of hardware accumulation. Mr. Loudon didn't even try. He was a stubborn and righteous man and couldn't believe the end would come, that the landlord to whom he had been paying rent for 38 years would suddenly refuse his check. It took a few weeks before Miss Coan persuaded him that the fate of the store was sealed,

194

that they had better give some thought to disposing of the stock. Admittedly it was hard to imagine what anyone would do with all that broken pyrex upstairs, the groaning shelves downstairs, together with the tide-soaked, decayed boxes and rusty containers. It was enough to make a saddened man chuckle a little just to think about it. There was enough useless material around to make a city look twice for a new dumping site.

One day some architects came in to look and measure. They said the building was going to be remodeled. Shops downstairs, offices up, with a grassed patio out in back. To Mr. Loudon it sounded like an impossible dream. A neat, clean grass patio out in back where all that junk is? What about those barrels of paint thinner? He shook his head in disbelief. He wouldn't accept it. But in a few more weeks he did. The realization broke his spirit. He went downhill in a hurry and never recovered.

The day before Mr. Loudon went to the hospital he asked your author to find another store to handle the hobby horse. Two generations of Sausalitans had ridden on it since it was first unpacked. It looked good enough for two more. John Minton, the proprietor of Creative Arts, was happy to have it. For a while the practice continued, but it was a losing attempt. Celebrating tourists have no feeling toward home town sentiment and traditions. They regarded the hobby horse as an oddity and laughed disrespectfully at it, stumbled over it, pushed it down the sidewalk, sat on it and generally abused the old veteran. Minton chained it to a parking meter, but received complaints that pedestrians were bumping into it. He had to put the old boy to pasture on his private deck at home and invite neighborhood children to ride.

Eight weeks after Mr. Loudon received the notice to vacate the building he was dead. Despite what the medical reports said, what really killed him was the worry and fretting over all his customers and how they would be taken care of.

The morning after his death someone placed a large green wreath on the door of the store.

Miss Coan was left to dispose of the stock. A difficult and pitiful task.

The closing of the hardware store was the death blow to residential services in the business district. There was no going downhill after that. The descent was over as far as residents were concerned. From then on, it was an entirely different show. Progress, perhaps.

Poor Mrs. Tew. There was so much trash left by so many people on the sidewalks she couldn't keep up with it. But she tried. Once a month she wore the rubber tip off her cane. Then she moved to Mill Valley, where she continued her civic cleansing operation.

The old hardware store was converted to another shop. The walls ring with memories. They once displayed utilitarian needs, but now are hung with Nordic nick-nacks and other enticements. But perhaps taxes are more important than tacks.

The intangible losses that residents suffered when a shop went out of business were, in some ways, as severe as the inconvenience caused by the loss. Hinges, paint, or shoe repair could be purchased in Mill Valley, three miles away. But when the personal element was lost it could never be regained. There were many little touches that helped make the town a good and pleasant place to live. But these attractions were being lost. Mr. Loudon, with his large, open face and kind laugh would say to a child standing in front of the counter:

"Put your hand up here." He'd touch the edge of the counter with his large but gentle hand. Hesitatingly the child would obey. Then suddenly Mr. Loudon would slap a piece of scotch tape across the little fingers. Surprise and delight. Always, after the initial experience, the child would look forward to the trick, and would never be disappointed.

Important? Who is to say? A town can survive without Mr. Loudons. But to the parent and the child the attention was significant. And anything that happens to a child is important.

Duke Enos quietly moved his plumbing shop one weekend in 1965. It was long overdue. The phone was a little more busy the past few years, but drop-ins were unheard of. Tourists passing his windows thought the shop was incongruous in the midst of bazaar, boutique and other gift shops. They'd stop and look and sometimes get a glimpse of Duke and his pipe in the back of the shop measuring or cutting pipe. He looked no different to them than their plumber back in Ohio. So Duke took his tools, pipes, fittings and kindness to the Gate 5 area. He wouldn't lose any customers. A phone call, and a half hour later he would be crawling beneath a house to remove a cleanout and clear the obstruction. He kept arteries to society reamed and flowing freely, and when necessary would perform a perfect shunt.

The building was vacant for a while after Duke left. The owner was asking an outrageous rent, and he could afford to wait until he got it. When a group of artists approached him he agreed to let them use the space for an art center on a month to month basis. They would have to pay utilities and insurance. For a while the artists wondered if they'd ever make the conversion. Years of plumbing grime covered the floor; dirt and oil compacted like a good macadam surface. But when they did get through the layers they discovered a marvelous ceramic tile floor laid on brick. The bricks were supported by a vaulted ceiling of the basement beneath. Beautiful arched cathedral-like construction that would be a credit to Christopher Wren.

When the art center got into operation, the group provided workshops and lessons, demonstrations and exchanges of ideas and guidance in various crafts, all on a voluntary basis. Some of the same people who started with Bern Porter. Enid Foster shared her subtleties, insights and techniques in painting; Mary Lindheim her expertise in pottery; Varda was unselfish with his knowledge, wit and talent. But the center's programs of performing arts were outstanding. Great artists in poetry, dance and drama came to display and teach. For the general public there were frequent performances of outstanding quality. Early in her career, Odetta came often to entertain a capacity audience with her clear, deep, soul voice that in turn could bring tears and laughter and chills to her listeners. Pete Seeger came one night. His appearance put a supreme test on the brick floor. The room couldn't hold one more person. Many who came couldn't get in. They lined the sidewalk outside to hear Pete's voice and message through the open door. He sang and played for hours. Children crowded at his feet. During intermission he drank a glass of water, then sat down on the front of the platform to entertain the children. Pete Seeger is a completely unselfish man. He has traveled the world over many times, teaching with his singing and his spirit one simple, but important message, "We're all in this together." Love. First comes love, with that there can be no big problems.

As always, and to be expected, the artists were unable to hold onto the building in the face of commerce and competition. The owner was offered the price he was asking for rental. A dime store went in, but it lasted less than a year. Then a man started converting it to a bookstore. Almost everyone in town thought the man was either an eccentric millionaire or a fool. A bookstore in Sausalito? The residents couldn't support it and tourists aren't looking for culture. But in a few years Herb Beckman proved they were all wrong, including himself. He never believed the store would be so successful. The Tides is the most popular business establishment in Sausalito. Its success is mainly due to ambiance. One feels something the moment one steps inside. It's there. Good vibes, as they say. If ambiance could be packaged, The Tides would have an exclusive commodity. Downstairs you can see the underside of the vaulted brick floor.

198

A sudden run of handmade jewelry stores sprang up in Sausalito. They crowded into corners of modish clothes stores, art galleries and any place that a small counter draped with a piece of black velvet could be placed. The creators of the new art craze realized the reputation Sausalito has as an artist's town, so they capitalized on the name. The first ones who came in were good artisans who created fine, delicate costume jewelry, each one different and distinct works of art. And then the followers came, getting on the bandwagon, turning out crude pieces of junk which they called jewelry. The 'things' they put together were made of easily workable wire, ponderous stones and misshapen metal with rough, sophomoric globs of solder binding them together. These were fobbed off as being artistic, unpolished, natural originals. Nonsense. They were rough and natural because there was no creative craftsmanship behind them. Many of the "creations" put together were revolting bulbous pendants that would look more at place in a hangman's den than around the neck of a beautiful woman. But they sold because they came from Sausalito.

32   There were many physical changes taking place in Sausalito in the early 1960s, but within city hall, behind the scenes, there were changes that shaped the town as much as shops and tourists. In the late '50s, Sausalito changed to a city manager form of government. This brought cries and criticisms from many old timers who believed the councilmen did it because they were incapable of running the town. It was a fair charge, but the town wasn't what it used to be. Sausalito became big business overnight. The budget doubled in two years after the Village Fair was built. Until 1958 the annual fluctuation was minimal and predictable. The small city hall staff could and did handle finances, assessments and all ancillary aspects of city business, with an occasional assist from the council. But a city manager is supposed to know all about the county, state and federal programs for money to build highways, parks, libraries, or of lease-purchase grants, urban renewal, and other programs. The city was losing out on grants and assistance available to qualified cities. Up to this time all excess money had been socked in a bank to draw a little interest, but a manager would know about investments to benefit the city more. So a manager was hired and the staff was relieved of a great amount of work and could spend more time on other aspects of a small town equally important. But they didn't like it. They had always run the whole show, now they were made stage hands. Some of them retired and took with them an invaluable amount of knowledge about Sausalito. A great loss. But Sausalito was changing fast. It could no longer chug along on an old magneto, it was generating new power too fast.

Miriam Ansell, the new clerk, was as precise as a computer and as confident as its answer. She was pleasing, pleasant and accommodating. Her face was as wide open as a child's, no subtleties, no mysteries. Her old-fashioned kind of honesty left her with no choice but to reveal anything and everything she knew about city government when a question was asked. "This is a democracy," she once said, "and what goes on in city hall is public knowledge." Later she protected herself by being more selective about what she learned.

The first city manager was a dour little man with business acumen in his veins, a no-nonsense man as close to a thinking machine as ever was put together. In his first year as manager he brought in eleven times his wages in financial aid from governmental agencies that the city had never before applied for. He was a business manager; Sausalito was in business and he was determined to make it profitable. To implement his programs, changes would have to be made in the town, but he wasn't hired to keep Sausalito a quiet little fishing village. With every assist or grant, however, there were conditions. To qualify for nearly a quarter of a million dollars to improve streets, the public works director had to be a licensed engineer. Paul Low had been public works director for twenty years and was doing an excellent job with five heavily-muscled men, a couple of wheel-barrows, picks and shovels and a truck. But Paul didn't have a diploma that attested to the fact that he could do what he had proved he could do. A quarter of a million dollars is a carrot of considerable attraction. It couldn't be resisted. The city hired an engineer who knew how to build and maintain roads because he had read it in books. Paul hadn't. He had been too busy building streets to crack a book. The new engineer had also been taught that to build streets properly, there would have to be heavy equipment. So backhoes, ditch diggers, graders, dump trucks and loaders were purchased. And then it followed that men were needed to operate this equipment. It would be foolish to buy it, then leave it idle. Two years after Mr. Low left, the budget for the public works department increased from $63,000 to $160,000. It is still growing, and all roads are paved.

The fire department is a good example of a unique situation in a small town. The greatest distance between city limits in Sausalito is two miles. From east to west it is much less. But Sausalito has two fire stations, both manned and equipped. A tremendous expense. This was necessary because there was but one road, Bridgeway, to get from one end of town to the other. Before tourist traffic, the fire truck could zip from the station at the north end of town to anywhere in Sausalito in minutes. But when the traffic became bumper to bumper from the business district to the Golden Gate Bridge, residents in old town, the south section, started complaining that they weren't getting adequate fire protection. They were right. A fire truck had to go up Princess Street and circle around narrow, winding streets to get to the southern portion, the route was slow and unpredictable. If a car was parked carelessly on Bulkley Avenue the truck couldn't get through. While it tried to maneuver, the house was burning. Because all residents are entitled to equal fire protection, a second station had to be built. In one year the budget tripled. In recent years the second station became an extravagance because of the widening of Bridgeway and the addition of an emergency lane.

The widening along the water's edge was a project not planned by the city, but it came about through a series of unrelated circumstances. The end product is good, and appears well planned, but credit should not be given to any bright visionary. It's like setting out to build a footstool and ending up with a rocking chair. It may be a good chair, but it wasn't what you expected. That smooth, wide unused emergency lane seems a little profligate to tourists as they sit bumper to bumper fuming in irritation while fighting the urge to swing onto it and move on. The lane wouldn't be there if it weren't for a governmental restriction. It came about in 1965 when it was discovered that the sea wall was crumbling along the waterfront, going back to the sea and carrying the roadbed with it. That portion of road takes a tremendous beating from upwards of 30,000 automobiles a week. The road had to be shored up. The town fathers got prices. The city couldn't afford it. The city manager made application to the state for help. The state said all right, but that the street would have to be made wider, because it has specifications, it can't be giving money to fix up just any street. The city said that was impossible. A wider street would be impractical. Sorry, said the state, we have our rules. In the meantime the street was slowly disintegrating. A dilemma: a bond issue to raise money, or accept state money and widen the street. Another carrot dangling.

During conferences with the state engineers, the city argued that to widen four hundred yards of a street would only make bottlenecks at both ends. Sausalito has enough problems as it is, we don't need to create more. "But," said the state, "our rules don't demand the extra width has to be used by the public. If it serves the public in some way, say on an emergency basis, it will satisfy our requirements."

It was after that remark that the fire chief suggested an emergency lane down the middle. This satisfied the state. It paid for almost all the expense, the city got the third lane and a better sea wall and roadbed because of state requirements.

There was much talk about how to distinguish the middle lane from traffic lanes, in order to keep the public off of it, before the idea of raising it was thought of. Even then there were doubts. One man suggested that at both ends a huge barrier be set in place. This barrier would look exactly like a heavy wooden beam, but be made of light plastic. Police and firemen would know it and drive right through. Hopefully motorists would never try.

Perhaps the biggest change behind the scenes that has occurred in Sausalito is in the police department. In 1958 there were twelve men on the police force; the budget was $50,000. In 1968 there were 22 men and the cost had risen to $272,000. In those ten years the population increased by only eight hundred people. The 1975 figures reveal the police budget is $725,000, up $453,000 in six years. There are four policemen per one thousand inhabitants. The national average is one per thousand.

But these are not fair comparisons. The reason for the large police force is the number of tourists. They have to be policed. Not all people who visit the town come to buy and gawk. Many come to case the town, to learn the possibility of burglary. They walk and ride over the hills and see the expensive homes hidden behind trees and shrubs. It all makes for privacy, but it has its disadvantages. Burglaries are a constant problem in Sausalito. As burglaries increased, so did complaints to city hall. More men were hired to patrol the streets. Unscheduled patrolling was tried but still the crime continued. So more men were hired and this required more patrol cars and more money added to the budget. But in addition to residential protection there was an increase in automobile moving violations. With 30,000 autos a week, there were many offenders of local laws. But the chief could handle that, if he had still more men. This wasn't difficult to effect.

204

The police department is the only city agency that makes money for the town. And no one knew this better than the chief. During the annual budget hearings he could and did justify all expenses he ever asked for.

The chief was young and scholarly, having walked the beat in a neighboring town only three years before his present appointment. He had attended all police schools and classes he could crowd in since getting out of the army. He took correspondence courses, wrote articles for trade journals, and always stressed the cerebral while saving shoe leather. The budget he presented one time in the '60s was forty pages long and so detailed you could accurately figure the water bill in the police station by the number of times the toilet was flushed. It was an astounding document that impressed the council. The chief had charts and figures which he pinned to a board. As he presented his arguments to justify hiring three more officers and buying two more patrol cars he had the confidence of water rushing through a broken dam. He was the expert.

"I have made studies," he said, "I know beyond a doubt that there are more than fifty moving violations per shift that the men can't apprehend because of the lack of manpower. This is wrong. As police chief, I must apprehend all violators of city ordinances and it hurts me to know I am not doing it. Furthermore, it is not right that some offenders are caught while others are not. These charts show you the revenue our department produced for the city last year and how much it can produce if we have the men and the cars. With these three men we will produce $30,000 annually, but more important we'll be protecting the written statutes in a fair and equitable manner."

The figures showed that from moving violations, over-time parking and court fines, the department in 1968 brought in $116,000. The chief was the expert, so very few questions were asked by the councilmen. Councilmen swear to uphold ordinances as does the chief. They had no choice and the request was granted.

As the number of tourists increased, so did the police department. In 1975 there were 29 men on the force. But they were producing revenue.

The danger of adding men by using the argument that the violators must be caught, is the instigation of a quota system. Each man must apprehend a certain number of violators. The chief has to justify the revenue he told the council he could produce. And he has been doing it. In 1975 the department brought $225,000 into the city's treasury from moving and overtime parking violations alone. But Sausalito had elevan lawsuits against it, charging that the victims were the result of the quota system. A Marin County grand jury investigation was made. Their verdict was yes and no. Insufficient proof. The chief denied having any such policy, but admits to telling his men that, "the violations are there. I know they are. If you're not bringing them in you're not doing your job."

But they've been doing their job, as thousands of visitors can attest. Moving violations are near the three thousand per year mark, parking and traffic citations are over ten thousand per year.

33 Most of the houses built in Sausalito before 1960 were built with lumber bought locally. The numerous visitors to Zack's popular restaurant don't realize that while sitting there good-timing-it-up they're either situated where a planing mill used to be or lolling over the ghost of the huge crosscut saw. Both were heavily used daily. After the Golden Gate bridge was built, a building boom began that kept that mill busy producing finished lumber. Zack's cocktail lounge sits over the spot where a huge chain saw was used to pull water-dripping logs from the bay. The view was mostly a vast area of corralled logs waiting their fate. Sucked up by the chain, they were quickly transformed into joists,

207

studs, beams and window sash. Now the view is of pleasure boats, mostly anchored, seldom used except for a symbol. The singing saw and whirring plane were familiar sounds in that area. The sounds contrast sharply to acid rock, amplifiers, automobiles and shouting celebrants. The odor of fresh cut lumber was a far cry from garlic bread and burned grease dripping on hot coals.

Directly across Bridgeway was another lumber yard. On the corner of Bridgeway and Turney street was the kiln where dried finish lumber was produced. In the '50s the building was Norberg's machine shop, and later Cassidy's plumbing shop; in the '60s a restaurant. It's fated to become part of a shopping complex. But it's not the first time that tourists and dollars have changed Sausalito's historic past to a doubtful future.

Until 1960, Sausalito had a city dump. It should still have one, and would, except for the competition it provided. The dump was located a quarter mile north of Zack's on property owned by an absentee landlord, who welcomed the fill. He should have been awarded a prize for offering harmless entertainment to the residents. But some merchants were complaining about the loss of business. Their attack was from the cosmetic angle, with sanitation thrown in under the guise of "we're only doing it for your own good." So the council ordered the area closed to the discarding of useful goods. After that it did become a dangerous, unsanitary bit of waterfront land. Rats took over and propagated profusely in the decaying debris. When it was a dump the residents kept it picked so clean no rats could survive.

This was not an ordinary city dump. The area was very small. It didn't take much space, because the dumping and hauling away about equalled each other. There was no attendant, yet order, respect and consideration was always displayed. As a man drove in he was usually met by a habitué of the dump.

208

"Hi. What ya got?"

"Oh, some lumber, a chair or two, an old sled, bed springs. I cleaned out my basement."

"Great. Let me look at it, will you?"

Frequently material was transferred from one trailer to another. Recycling has always made sense.

If no one was around, the discards were placed with other, similar material.

A side asset to the dump was the number of friendships made while rummaging for surprises. Many of these friendships became life long. A warm summer evening often found a half dozen or so people looking over the treasures, talking, exclaiming, enjoying themselves.

"Hey, here's an old waffle iron. Let's put that aside for Bud. He likes to fix things like that." Cooperation. Any lumber four feet long or more had many takers. There's a house in Sausalito affectionately called "The Little Dumpling" because so much of the lumber used in building it came from the dump. That house sold for $35,000 in 1969, which put it out of the shack class.

During the late '50s, the city decided it was getting too sophisticated to have a dump, and the pressure increased from businessmen downtown. "Our waterfront is our most cherished heritage," it was agreed, "and to have part of it cluttered with junk is a disgrace and a waste." So they erected a fence and attached authoritative signs. The recycling stopped. Basements became cluttered. Backyards piled high with brush. Fire hazards increased. The land is still vacant. Since the closing of the dump the Salvage shop has received more goods and the refuse company more business.

In 1970 the townspeople approved a bond issue to purchase the old city dump land on which to build a library and city hall. On the same ballot they voted against the money to erect the buildings. Civic progress, if any, goes in slow, easy stages in Sausalito. So the city owned the land but it had no money with which to build the complex. The area lay absolutely unused for several years, then in 1974 a group of volunteers made a waterfront park out of it. Plants and sod were donated by a local group of Sausalito Artists and Merchants, who have an acronym that sounds nationally patriotic: SAM. The area is named Dunphy Park. Earl Dunphy has contributed more time to public service than any other person in Sausalito. Using the land for a public park is a much better use than a city hall complex. The city council will get the credit for the park, even though it set out to do something else and failed. It's not the first time. Perhaps councils should have a monument to failure.

34 Sausalito was one of the few cities in America which refused Carnegie money to build a library. The council at the time acted wisely and quickly in refusing. Everyone in town was so pleased with the library they had that it was unthinkable to consider a change. The council might as well have been asked if they wanted more air to breathe; they didn't need it.

In 1937 Mabel Wosser took over the reins as librarian, following her sister's retirement. Another sister was a library trustee. In fact it was frequently referred to as the Wosser Library. No matter what it was called, it was a good library in more ways than merely providing books. It had atmosphere, some would say, but whatever the description, many residents frequently went to the library with no particular thought or book in mind. It was a homey, quiet, peaceful and friendly refuge. All credit for the club-like feeling goes to Mabel Wosser, and the few clerks she employed.

To start the day, Miss Wosser would choose some flowers from her garden at her birthplace on Pine St., then walk to the library where she threw out the day-olds and arranged the fresh. If any books had been delivered, she unpacked them, and laid away certain titles until she could phone a patron or two and notify them that a book had come in that she thought they would like. Withholding them from the public didn't bother her conscience. She did it so frequently that most residents had received the special consideration at one time or another. About once a month she'd go to San Francisco with a large shopping bag to purchase books direct.

All of the clerks in the library were insatiable readers. When they read a book that they knew would interest a certain patron, they too laid the book aside and called the reader.

Patronage increased every year that Miss Wosser was librarian. Children, especially, used the reference room frequently, where the clerks encouraged and aided them in their research for written reports.

There were many hard-core patrons who spent hours every day in the library. Clerks could tell who was coming up the stairs by the sound of their footsteps. These patrons were so familiar with the physical layout they knew where squeaks in the floor were located, and would avoid the area so as not to disturb readers.

The city council never gave the library a thought except at budget time, when Miss Wosser would present an amount she said was needed to operate the library for the coming year, and they would grant it. It was the only department in the city that functioned with absolute predictability from one year to the next. The library didn't cost much to operate. In 1940 the budget was $3,686.00 for books, salaries and maintenance. Some of the low cost could be attributed to the dedication of the help. They were people who loved books and felt it a privilege to be surrounded by them.

In 1965 Miss Wosser retired after nearly thirty years as librarian, to spend more time in her garden and home and to be with her family and friends. The library has not settled down since then. There have been five librarians and several periods of interim chiefs in nine years, each of whom instigated her system, her method of doing things. This has had a disheartening effect on the library. There are books, but gone is the atmosphere, the ambiance, the good vibes. The new librarians were well educated and had degrees to prove it. But it was mostly book training. They sat in a small office poring over graphs and lists and reading the latest trade journals. They never worked at the circulation desk and seldom met any patrons. They knew the Dewey decimal system and how to look up reference questions and where to find lists of newly published books. With one exception, they weren't readers. But they knew which books were on the shelves because they had ordered them and they could defend their selection by the lists; New York said they were good books.

In 1967 an active library board and an energetic librarian decided that Sausalito should have a new library. Within a few months enthusiasm was at a high pitch throughout town, and the momentum couldn't be stopped. It was amazing how, in such a short time, many residents who had never given the library a thought, suddenly became interested and convinced that the need was there. Actually the library was so old that most people thought it was time to have a new one. It's true, the building was getting weak and tired. The building inspector warned that no more weight be added with books, or they'd all end up downstairs in city hall. Some plaster had already fallen from the ceiling. Council meetings were held in trepidation. During a meeting some people in the know kept looking skyward, not for guidance, but for their safety. The city was able to build; there was nearly a hundred thousand dollars in a fund, which had been set aside by a five cent override library tax during the past twenty years. The librarian and the board were eager to spend the money. They decided on a structure costing $425,000. A bond election was set.

During the campaign there were two issues; the waterfront location on the Sandspit next to the main parking lot, and the size of the building. Many people were totally against blocking views of the waterfront. The argument against that was that the land was free and the area would be open to the public anyway. Another group said, "It's too large. We don't need a library of congress. The population hasn't increased more than a thousand in ten years. Why have a library five times the size we've got? Just think of what it will cost to maintain that big fancy building."

But the librarian had convinced the council the need for a large building was there. The public wasn't convinced, and the bond lost by 195 votes, on three main grounds: 1. The waterfront location; 2. The size; 3. Deception. The contention was that neither operational nor janitorial services would increase. Many people knew better. They feared their taxes would go up.

The council was irked, but not stopped. The law required a two-thirds majority to approve the bond issue. Far more than half of the residents favored it. "This is government by minority," it was said. The council decided to build the library anyway. They could do it by a lease-purchase arrangement. It wouldn't have to go to a vote. This decision aroused another camp of opponents. They thought the council was being arrogant and dictatorial. In effect the council was saying, "We're going to build despite the vote."

The delay allowed more people to become interested in the situation. It was learned, for example, that only a few favored architects had been invited to submit plans for the building. They were all good architects, but many residents thought there should have been wide-open competition for the job. But the library board wanted a name. An aroused public forced a referendum election. Before it went to vote the plans were revised, some frills deleted, the size diminished. It lost by 45 votes.

It was a victory for the Sausalito Citizens' Council. A great loss to many hard working, dedicated people who had more interest in culture and the future of Sausalito than concern over a few dollars increase in their taxes. But the issue was dead. A disappointed council gave up.

A long dry spell continued after that. Each succeeding librarian was promised a new library to be built somewhere. But as each location was rejected for some reason or another, the librarians resigned. "There'll never be a new library," they said. Costs were rising, and the board couldn't agree on a site.

A new council in 1968 had an opportunity for a new library that would have cost less than the $100,000 sitting in the bank, but they passed it up.

A plan was presented to them to purchase the Charles Van Damme, a familiar ferry on the Sausalito waterfront, move it to the foot of Johnson St., behind the post office, where pilings would be driven around it and sand pumped in to float the vessel. This is a well-known method of preserving and stabilizing ships. The ferry would then be converted to a library three times the size of the old one. The huge stack would be made into a fireplace. Open decks would be inviting for summer reading. The old side-wheeler had historic value and would be worth conserving. The land belonged to the city. Architects who inspected the ferry agreed with the plan. The librarian was enthusiastic for it. It would be a unique library, and a fitting one for a waterfront town.

The council was skeptical. Perhaps the idea should have been presented to them in slow stages; for it took them by surprise. None of them had ever believed there was a solution to the library question that wouldn't cost at least a quarter of a million dollars. This was too simple. The skepticism suddenly made nautical engineers, long range planners, architects and traffic experts out of the council.

"No one has ever heard of a library on a ferry," said one. "It's on the wrong side of Bridgeway," said another, "it wouldn't be safe for children." "I looked it over, and frankly I don't believe it's in good enough condition," was another remark.

"If it's not in good condition," said the proponent, "I wouldn't want it either. So I'll make a motion that the city hire a marine surveyor to learn its physical condition. If he says 'No,' that will be the end of it."

"How much will the survey cost?"

"Two hundred fifty dollars."

"It's money down the bilge," said one councilman.

"The residents wouldn't go for it. They want a new building," said one.

"I think it's worth a try," said Jan Dyk, and seconded the motion.

A vote was taken. The motion lost three to two.

The ferry, at this writing, still stands at Gate 6. She's deteriorating fast. She could have been a proud vessel still serving the public in a useful way.

After the 1970 attempt for a new library failed, the city purchased an old school house that was abandoned by the district and declared unsafe in many areas. The building was converted to a library and city hall. It's an older building than the ferry. But it's square looking and more conforming. Perhaps it's what Sausalito deserves.

35 Sausalito has been as proud of its waterfront as if the city fathers had invented land, sea and tides. There has been much desecration over the years to parts of it, but much protection too. In fact, the zealous guarding of the Richardson Bay shoreline has often reached selfish and unreasonable heights. People living on the waterfront quickly learned if they wanted to build a dock or a houseboat, the only way to do it was to do it, and don't ask questions. If you seek a permit you'll stir up city hall enough to add a whole new department to its government. No one knew this better than Delmar Wise. In 1965 Delmar, who owned a ship repair business at the foot of Napa Street, brought in four huge dry docks and moored them out in the bay 300 yards from Sausalito's sacrosanct shores. Parking them there permanently was not his plan, but their presence created enough irritation in city hall to produce perfect pearls. In 1975 the dry docks were still there. Many people thought of them as huge, obdurate and defiant monsters, an ugly lumpy brooding sentinel with nothing to watch. At one

217

time they were considered a danger to navigation because they sat in the middle of a deep channel. But they were not a danger because their presence prohibited large boats from passing, and small boats could easily see them.

One calm and peaceful night in 1965, the city council was in session, with Mayor Mel Wax spearheading various discussions. The council had just heard a report from a committee on the number of illegal houseboats tied up at various docks and was pleased to learn there were only eleven: the sanctity of the waterfront was not endangered. The overall report of the waterfront was cheering. While the report was being heard Delmar Wise stepped out of his favorite bar fifty feet from city hall and watched two of the huge hulks move silently and stealthily into position. He smiled, then stepped back into the bar and ordered a double. The council went home at midnight content that city staff was on the job.

In the morning the city, councilmen included, awoke to see the structures sitting there in low tide mud. The entire town was upset. Many residents blamed city hall for allowing the obstructions. The city manager sent the building inspector to learn who the docks belonged to and who was responsible. He didn't learn a thing; Delmar Wise was home nursing a well earned hangover.

Two weeks went by while citizens engaged in enough discussion to solve world disarmament and got nowhere. The structures were worth talking about, just by their size alone. Each one was 100 feet long, 50 feet wide and 40 feet high. Tied together, they took up considerable space. The council met again expecting city staff to answer all questions, and the staff was waiting for council instruction. They got it. But while the meeting was taking place, the tide was high, conditions were favorable, so Delmar Wise moved in two more dry-docks. It was getting so it didn't pay to hold council meetings.

When Wise was finally contacted, he said his plan was to bring the docks into his repair yard, overhaul them and sell
218

them to the navy. But first he would have to dig a channel to his yard. He was going to seek a dredge permit from the Corps of Engineers. As soon as that was done he would move them in, one at a time, and do the work. The repair would take a month on each one. Six weeks went by with no activity. The city checked with the Corps of Engineers and learned that no application for dredging had been applied for. A talk with Wise brought vague answers. The city then passed an ordinance prohibiting repair of vessels over 25 feet high and 50 feet long. Now the city had him; he would have to remove the controversial docks.

Mr. Wise didn't oppose the ordinance, which piqued the council. But Wise couldn't be bothered. He had no specific plans anyway. He had bought the huge docks at a bargain and was going to leave them out there until a deal came along. It didn't cost him anything for storage. Months went by. The city ordered him to remove the docks. "They're outside city limits," he responded. "The city has no jurisdiction over that area." So the city requested the county to deal with Wise. It took months for the county to respond. When it did, it said that because the docks were in navigable waters, the coast guard would be responsible. In nine months the coast guard responded. A thick document arrived. "Ah, now we've got him," thought the authorities. "This has the stamp of the U.S. Government." Then it was read. After wading through verbosity, the report concluded in stiff-upper-lip phrases which, interpreted, said, "The channel is not navigable enough to come under our jurisdiction. It's up to the county."

By now a year and a half had passed and the drydocks were becoming a familiar fixture on the Sausalito scene. Many people liked them, others didn't mind one way or another, but city hall was irritated. Legally the city could do nothing, and complaints to the county had little effect because the county as a whole wasn't bothered by the structures. Occasionally though, the supervisors would discuss the situation

219

and newspaper accounts would be written telling of the board's sympathy with Sausalito. In the meantime the dry docks were making themselves permanent in the muddy bottom of the bay. Each time the tide went out, their heavy bulk settled them deeper until they were a quarter of the way in the mire.

It was another year before the county got into the debacle again. The city complained of the number of hippies living on the structures. The county investigated and indeed found a small colony well established, living peacefully, with almost all comforts found in land-located houses. Central heat and wall-to-wall carpets were missing, but so were taxes and upkeep. Sanitation was no problem; a hole cut in the deck with a 20 feet drop to tide-flushing waters served the purpose. There was privacy, except from high powered binoculars behind the windows of wealthy voyeurs and scatological-minded home owners on the hills. But many people who were secure enough in their own lives not to be jealous of others', enjoyed the idea of people living out there if they wanted to. The clothes lines with colorful garments, a curl of smoke from primitive cooking arrangements made a peaceful scene. But it was against the rules. It took much policing to enforce the eviction that was served, frequent trips in a boat, confrontations, disagreeableness. "But we're not hurting anyone and the owner said we could stay here."

"I can't help it. You have to live the way the county wants you to live," said the process server.

It was a foolish bureaucratic order. The inhabitants were not conformists. They would dwell in another location in much the same way they were living on the docks. The county couldn't abate and abolish the people, but it was good at harrassing.

The county continued its pursuit. There was a new group of supervisors by now, and they were going to clean up loose ends of the old administration. An official order came to Wise. "Remove the dry docks within 60 days or the county will do it and bill you for the costs."

Wise's answer: "I don't own them any more." He was not a communicative man, so it took several months to learn that Chris Roberts was the new owner. Chris was a Gate 5 inhabitant, a sculptor, talker, dreamer who lived in a hand-made houseboat at the end of Jon's ferry. The authorities who thought Wise was difficult were soon to get a lesson in obstinacy.

The county threatened Chris with removal costs, but the letter got only slightly better treatment than third class mail; Chris read it before tossing it into the fireplace. He knew the county wouldn't incur such an expense unless it could recover the money. Chris had none. His only assets were a used car and a sinking houseboat. Instead of thinking of flotation for his own home, he was dreaming of grandiose schemes for the dry docks. He would bring the four docks into Gate 5, tie them together and make a unique performing arts center. There were to be high arched, gracefully curved roofs covered with clear plexiglass, sunken areas, art galleries, huge open fireplaces, numerous stages, work areas for different crafts, orchestra pits and a concert hall acoustically sound, and dreams, dreams, dreams. But alas! He couldn't get financial backing. Chris was discouraged but kept trying, which was more than the county could say. It gave up. In the meantime a few of the people who had been evicted from the docks retaliated for the harrassment they had received by rowing out to the docks in the dead of night and painting a 30 foot bright yellow and white daisy on the side facing Sausalito, beneath it the word LOVE.

Everybody had waited too long; the drydocks could no longer be floated. But they served a purpose in the long chain of events. Countless numbers of teredo colonies have fed on the wood, thus keeping alive that particular marine termite. The docks settled more and more into the mud as the insects devoured. At one time the county decided to burn the structures, but a more powerful government body refused permission. "The heavily creosoted lumber would pollute the atmosphere," said the Air Pollution Control Board. A fire was purposefully set on the docks one night, and did considerable damage until the Sausalito Fire Department's marine unit extinguished it. That was the only time in history that city hall was displeased with the department's efficiency.

The deterioration of the docks has been slow. A few boards have been ripped off from time to time when needed by enterprising waterfront dwellers; a good cause. After a decade a salvage company offered to dismantle the docks for the spoils. It will be done; another case of profit doing what bureaucracy couldn't do.

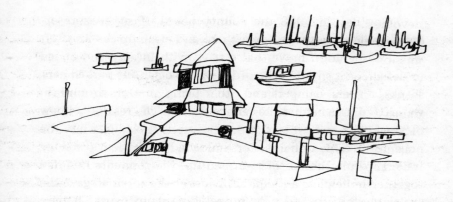

36 The houseboat colony in the Gate 5 area has always been a thorn in the side of Sausalito. A few tickles, laughs and amusement are there for community joviality, but officially the council would like to have the entire area drop into the bay. But having no influence over miracles, or legal authority over the area because it is outside the city limits, the council has exerted influence on county agencies to clean up the area and change the residents' life style. A big order. All their efforts have been a waste of time, like pleading with the snails in your garden. Elected officials don't like eclectic residents, and Gate 5 least of all. The sanitary board, for example, will not allow the houseboats to connect to public sewers. Perhaps their sewage will not meet the board's standards. But not allowing hookups, then blaming them for dumping raw sewage into the bay is a typical government inconsistency. The board gives as an excuse the substandard building practices in the area. Other pressures come in the form of harassment from the county building inspector and the sheriff.

One day in 1968 the county board of supervisors ordered bulldozers to 'go down there and clean up the area.' It was a desperation move that started with infamy and ended in defeat, as it should. The order was to clear out parked cars, shacks, trailers, campers and other living quarters around the waterfront area behind the service station. The residents knew of the order and were waiting early one morning when the huge, formidable iron monsters unloaded from their low slung trailers. While the motors warmed up, the residents huddled together in helpless anticipation. Just as the foreman gave the signal to start, several people, including women with babies, sat down in front of the awesome blades, their backs to the destroyers. It was enough to melt the heart of a bulldozer operator. They couldn't, wouldn't move. After this failure there was unsettled peace for a long period. But it didn't last. The next show occurred out in the waters, and as predicted, just a month before election. The supervisors seeking reelection wanted to demonstrate to constituents that they meant business about cleaning up Gate 5. What they did this time was dramatic and costly. Their attempt was to remove all floating houseboats that were encroaching on underwater streets. A large tug boat was rented, a crew assembled; sheriff's deputies and process servers armed with court approved injunctions were present. When high tide came one day the pirates set out. The first houseboat they chose was the last. They moved in as close as they could and one of the deputies informed the occupants why they were there. No response, except a humping of the shoulders. When the men on the tug felt they were close enough they tossed the loop of a heavy hawser across a few feet of open space toward a cleat on the deck of the houseboat. It missed and fell into the muddy water. The men hauled it up and tried again, and again, cursing all the while.

The occupants of the houseboat, one a young man dressed in ripped off jeans just above the knees, and nothing

224

else, bearded, long haired, one ear ring dangling, stood in a doorway drinking coffee. He moved just enough to allow his woman to stop through the door as a mumu fell over her naked body.

"What's up?" she asked.

"The fuzz," he replied, shrugging.

"Oh."

She sat down on a saw horse and ran her fingers through her long straight hair as if to comb the sleep away.

The deputies in their form fitting epauletted shirts, knife edged trousers and precisely tilted caps, had an expression that was closer to disrespect and hate than it was to tolerance and kindness. The houseboat dwellers didn't exactly love the deputies either, but the contrast in contempt was marked. The deputies hated the houseboat people because of their life style, they wanted to change it. Gate 5 residents neither cared how other people lived nor tried to inflict their standard on others. A standoff of mutual disrespect.

At last the loop ringed the cleat and the slack was taken up. The court order was tossed onto the deck where it remained. The two occupants continued what they were doing, totally unperturbed. When the order was given the tug gunned its motor and off it went pulling hawser and cleat behind. The cleat had been bolted to old rotten wood and was unsafe to use or a line would have been tied to it to anchor. The tug, with its thousand horse power marine engine, looked foolish dragging rope after it. The cleat had sunk to the bottom. The scene provided a few laughs from the houseboat colony.

The next attempt was also a failure. This time the men looked the houseboat over carefully and selected a strong anchorage. When they moved in close, the man on the houseboat pushed them off with a long pole. Twice the loop did get over the post, but before the slack was taken up, it was lifted off and dropped into the water. Hundreds of people had lined the waterfront watching the sea battle, cheering the defenders and jeering the oppressors. Photographers were present having a field day. The scene ended when a deputy couldn't stand the frustration and the jeering and did the only thing he knew. He reached for his gun and threatened the two on the houseboat. This signaled the marine inspector to call off the whole show before serious trouble occurred. The tug and its crew moved off like a whipped dog.

Following these incidents, a few waterfront people were talking in Dan Logan's houseboat. The discussion centered around what the authorities might try next. Dan would know, if anyone did. He had been living on the waterfront since the days when sea gulls outnumbered the people in the area; long before the shipyard was built, and before science declared that human waste polluted the sea. Dan had seen enough harassment to shatter a stone. He had survived it all, with spiritual guidance from homemade gin. His face showed the scars of many bottles. Frequently his sense of humor cost him dollars in grief; even if he knew it would, he'd follow his plan just for the laugh. But Dan could be serious and often was. He had time to think and used the time.

Varda started the conversation. "It is impossible to know what they might do next because they are not logical. It is their best weapon."

"Certainly," said Dan, "and they will continue. Their tricks are bureaucratic banderillas inflicted by political picadors. Before we are weakened any more, we must strike back. Take the offensive with a plan. If we know what we are doing, it will put them off guard."

"Precisely," said Varda, "but we must make sense, be consistent and logical, for they won't know how to handle that. At the same time our scheme should be so clever it will be impossible, for impossibility is the only thing they understand."

"Exactly," said Dan.

"You have been thinking, Dan," said Varda. "What profundity has your nimble mind evoked on the subject?"

226

"Dreams."

"They are the best. What dreams? Tell us."

"To save Sausalito before it devours itself. If we do that we can save our community."

"Good. That is the impossibility we are looking for. Tell us more."

"You must remember that before Sausalito became a tourist attraction, the town exerted no pressure on the waterfront people. Sausalito didn't care about us. Oh, they knew we existed and they derived a certain amount of popularity because of us. They even thought enough of us to give us a name, but they treated us anonymously, which was all right with us. But now that the town is a success, it has taken on different values and can no longer stand our looks, our behavior, our existence. Money does that to people. And so Sausalito must be decommercialized before it becomes dehumanized."

"Bravo," exclaimed Varda. "Miracles are acceptable, and are usually performed by common men. How would you perform this one, our leader?"

Dan laughed, then continued.

"It is not too difficult. We organize only enough to show our sincerity, but not enough to show our strength. That is to say, we request annexation to Sausalito and demonstrate enough responsibility to impress the governing board that we wish to become useful human beings and are anxious to become part of the system, so to speak. When that is accomplished, we really do organize and elect enough councilmen to have a majority. There are many sympathetic hill people who will be on our side, for they want their town back. Then we select a mayor who will proclaim that all public parking lots downtown be turned into public parks. One small area to be reserved for free resident parking. Then we will remove all parking meters from public streets and prohibit parking there. By getting rid of the automobiles, we will be preventing most violations of our city laws. We must do this. It is not right for a municipality to invite and encourage cars, then make laws against them. Our traffic laws are violated hundreds of times daily. Therefore we must get to the source of the trouble; prevent crime. We either get rid of the laws or the autos, but we cannot be unreasonable, so the laws must remain, the autos must go. Yes, it's true there will be a tremendous loss of revenue from parking fines and other traffic violations, but that will be offset by reducing the police force to less than one quarter of its present size. We won't need them. No autos, no violations. Indeed the citizens should not be paying for the large police force that now exists; the merchants should, for it is the shops that attract the people who have to be policed. In a sense they are special police, their sponsors should pay the expense. The American people have a symbiotic relationship with their automobiles; they cannot detach themselves from them for long and survive. When they learn they can no longer come to Sausalito and leave their cars within a very short distance from their destination, they will not come. And then, what will follow? The inevitable. Rents will start falling in the shopping area first. When they get low enough, a shoe repair shop will return, a hardware store, a toy store, a hobby horse. The park will be returned to citizen use and familiar faces will be seen downtown once more. And won't it be good to see a child or two with a bamboo fishing pole over his shoulder, heading for the uncrowded waterfront?"

37   In a small town like Sausalito, a good yardstick of any significant change taking place is the budget. Generally where there's no great population increase, the budget doesn't change much from year to year except for inflation. Not so in Sausalito. But there are reasons which we'll mention later. Budgets are figures which can be as boring as a bit, but a quick look at some budgets will reveal another side of Sausalito, not seen by tourists.

In 1955 the population of Sausalito was 4,945, and it cost $232,000 to operate the town. This was just three years prior to the Village Fair and the tourist invasion. The 1975 census showed 6,170 residents, a rise of 1,225, but the budget was two million six hundred dollars. Why? Mainly tourists. And where did all the money go? Salaries mostly. In 1955 combined salaries for the entire city amounted to $117,000. In 1975 a million and three quarters. That's a far cry from the days when city hall was run by a clerk and a few helpers. It would seem that Sausalito was out to prove Parkinson's Law. The little town is top heavy with administrative personnel. For example, the town covers only two square miles, and nearly all of that is built on.

Part of the old shipyard is left, and in the throes of development. Yet the city employs a planner, an assistant planner, an administrative aide, two planning interns and a stenographer to grind out all the paper work. One can see why the stenographer is necessary.

The charge that Sausalito is a rich little town is not true. The revenue in 1973 exactly matched the costs to operate for the year. In 1975 it is expected to have slightly over $40,000 in excess. Not very much. Spending every dollar it makes takes some doing. So far it's been successful. Not much different from many imprudent households.

The census figures do not reflect the population explosion that occurs every day in Sausalito. In the summer months 20,000 people a day come to Sausalito by ferry, auto, boats and bicycles. It costs money to control and manage that many people. We've shown how the police department grew, and why it had to. It's much the same with the public works department. There's a tremendous amount of wear and tear on the streets from automobiles. The streets have to be maintained. Every morning in the wee silent hours, Bridgeway and the sidewalks are washed, using expensive equipment. Another man empties all litter cans. The amount of debris left by tourists is staggering. Bridgeway is the dining room for all the carry out food stores. The city pays for the janitorial service. All day long a man walks the sidewalks picking up fish-and-chips paper, tacos wrappers, left over hot dog napkins and pounds of carelessly thrown refuse. If this constant policing wasn't done Bridgeway would look like a New Years eve celebration by the end of the day, every day. We've seen why the fire department had to build another station. That department's costs rose from $38,000 in 1955 to over $500,000 in 1975. No one begrudges the cost. It's an outstanding department that stresses and teaches fire prevention. It's rare that a truck leaves the station for a fire.

Another important department in every town is the

library. Here again are some tell-tale figures. In 1955 it cost $12,500 to run the entire library including all salaries and purchase of books. In 1975 the chief librarian alone got $17,800, plus fringe benefits. The department's budget was $95,000 for the year. Salaries amount to $60,000. These are particularly interesting figures in that tourists do not affect a library operation. A few wander in asking for a rest room. Some sit down to read and rest. But they can't take out books. Statistics show that in 1931 the average book circulation per day was about the same as 1975, so the library wasn't as busy per capita as it used to be. Perhaps people walked and read more in the past. Today they depend upon their cars, and it is too much trouble to fight traffic. But now that the library is established in the old school that was renovated for the purpose, patronage will pick up.

Despite the costs that tourists incur, they also provide money. Sausalito is being paid for the loss of the town to outsiders. A few residents wondered if it was worth it, but they realized there was no stopping the metastasis of merchandising. "Sausalito is where the transaction is," became the slogan.

Most towns operate mainly on revenue derived from property taxes. Sausalito did so until the late 1950s, but now the automobile is the greater source. Property taxes in 1975 amounted to $700,000. A large sum for a small town. But the automobile brings in more money than houses. In 1975 the projected figure of revenue from the automobile was $804,000. These dollars will come from parking, meters, fines, licenses and gas taxes.

People bring automobiles, and while the iron monster is eating up parking time, the people are spending money. The city can't lose. Those who come by ferry also contribute to the treasury in sales taxes. In 1975 the merchants collected and paid $597,000 to the city through sales taxes, business licenses and other related items.

231

But how were residents reacting to the rapid commercialization? Most carped, but all paid heavily in other ways besides dollars for the loss of their town. They paid in inconvenience. The traffic was nearly intolerable. Should a citizen need something from downtown, he would have to allow a half hour fighting traffic to get there. He planned his day and chores for early morning. But there were fewer and fewer resident-serving businesses downtown; they were being crowded out by high rent gift shops. So residents had less reason to use their town. In 1975 there were 900 business licenses in Sausalito, with less than a dozen useful to residents. This explains a sad phrase one hears spoken by residents; "Oh, I never go downtown anymore. I can't remember when I was last down there." Shopping for essentials was done in nearby communities. "Shop local," may be a good slogan for most towns, but in Sausalito it was impossible. Some relief came when the council voted to allow residents to park free in the city owned parking lots. The problem was getting to the lots. But it did help citizen morale. All they needed was a sticker on their windshields proving they were residents and they could drive into a parking lot free. It was a small jab at tourists. Then some citizens wanted to go a step further. They petitioned the council to allow stickered cars to park free in metered areas on the streets. They argued that there would be no loss in income to the city and more convenience to residents. Shop owners liked it too, for it would get residents downtown. But the campaign didn't get far.

"Discrimination," said the city attorney. "The city doesn't own the streets. The state does. They're public property. If you let Sausalito residents park free you have to let everyone."

It was a good idea until the workability was investigated. However, residents still get two hours free parking in the lots. A council would be dead if it tried to take that away from them. A small black market distribution of duplicated stickers

232

was started, but it made very little money.

The city council boasts that the property tax rate in Sausalito has increased only ten cents per hundred assessed valuation in fifteen years. It's true, but it's a meaningless sum. Property taxes have increased an average of 500% in that period, and that's real money. The average tax per house in Sausalito in 1975 was $1,700.00 per year. This is very hard on pensioners and old timers who built their modest houses for future security. They are the ones who made the town, and who have, over the years, paid thousands of dollars to the treasury to pave the streets, to build a police and fire department, to support the library, in an effort to make a community for themselves and their children. Many of their homes cost under $2,000 to build, but in 1975 the average house was valued at $75,000. Taxes have to be paid on that value, and it is impossible for many to meet that expense. They not only lost their town to tourism but some lost their homes as well. They were forced to sell and move away from friends and neighbors. And why was this allowed to happen? Because it couldn't be stopped. Sausalito is a desirable place to live for many people, and there aren't many houses to live in. This creates demand. The newer inhabitants use Sausalito for different reasons than the old residents did. People with money who want to live there will pay nearly any price. This increases valuation. Steep hillside lots that a mountain goat would think twice before attacking sell for $45,000 each. It's expensive building on these lots, but the higher the cost the more taxes. If a man can afford it and doesn't mind paying, the city is happy to get the money.

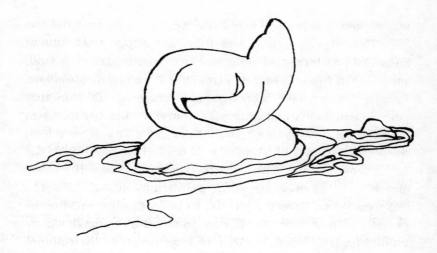

38 City council races bring out enough inconsistencies and confusion to stir the soul of the great political writer H. L. Mencken. Perhaps that is the way it should be. Stirring the pot occasionally brings up meat and flavor. Sausalito seems to create big stews, with enough side dishes to make rijstafel.

The basis of confusion stems mostly from residents not being able to come to grips with reality by admitting that Sausalito is a tourist attraction. Candidates have to defend the village concept to be elected. Businessmen who have run for a seat have been defeated. Their charge is always the same, "The councils in the past have been trying to run business out of the city." They want to change that direction. Opponents claim the councils have sold out to commercialism. They want to prevent it. Some say the town needs someone in there who will stir things up. Another side says we don't need agitation, we need councilmen who will settle problems, not create new ones. There was a time in the past when candidates differed on how to solve problems, but now no two candidates can agree on what the problems are. But there is one point of agreement: council meetings are as long-winded as an air tunnel and just as void.

Why anyone wants to be a councilman in the first place is a mystery, for it's a thankless post that carries four years of bondage to monotonous meetings filled with indecisions and obfuscations. If a man is decisive, quick minded, business-like, and "wants to get on with it," he's in for frustration, or a change in nature. After three hours of discussion and indecision on a subject, councilmen usually put it off until next meeting. But they are consistent. They took an equal amount of time and talk to change the entire zoning ordinance as they did to decide on a new flag pole after the old one had been devoured by termites. Pettiness and jealousies seem to be in big favor among councilmen and women. There are some who vote against their better judgment because the vote they prefer would favor an enemy on the other end of the table. The city suffers as a result. But the worst part of being a councilman in Sausalito is that most problems are not related to a small town. Until 1958, almost all items on the agenda affected someone in town directly. But currently 75 per cent of meeting time is spent in trying to solve problems created by automobiles and commerce. A councilman today works mostly for the businessmen, trying to solve problems to make business in town run more smoothly.

"Let's keep Sausalito a residential village" was a slogan used by all councilmen until the late '60s. But no longer. The last time that philosophy was used was in 1968, during one of the biggest issues Sausalito had faced in many years.

A mile north of downtown was an old distillery, which burned in 1963. It was located on a choice 14 acre piece of land, gerrymandered so it was not in the city limits. The distillery provided 60 jobs to local residents, and other joys to many more. Many part-time workers were employed who stayed on the job long enough to stock themselves with spirits for the duration of unemployment. It was the only fringe benefit available. Some who were more cagey at cadging sold the goods to regular customers. It was a great spiritual loss to the community when 200,000 gallons of alcohol went up in flames. The land was sold, cleared and made ready for a development. After it was annexed to the city, the owner applied for permission to build a "swinging singles" apartment complex. No one over 30 to be allowed, no legally married couples need apply. It was a natural for Sausalito. But the councilmen in 1968 were still thinking, "residential community." It was an ostrich position, vulnerable and indefensible.

Rumors abounded and phone calls to councilmen expressing opinions ran at a great rate. The city hall chambers were filled on the night of the hearing. Citizens by the dozens spoke against the application, hinting that anyone who approved was immoral, sinful and condemned to hell. It was an amazing display of "better than thou" attitude. To give permission to such goings on would be tantamount to allowing "Deep Throat" to be shown at the weekly teen club movie night. The council was aware that other governing bodies had ruled on *how* people should perform on percales, but they were being asked *who* should. Fortunately David Freedheim, the president of the school board, spoke against the application with the only sensible reason heard. He cited figures that showed the district was losing children, when it should be gaining. He favored large apartments, playgrounds and part commercial development in order to attract families with children. He went on to say that Sausalito needs people who will participate in civic affairs, to serve on boards and commissions, and that it was far more likely that men and women with families would stay longer and be more active in the community than singles who were more apt to be transient. It was logical and gave the council a sound reason to disapprove the application, which was voted down unanimously. They were still thinking of saving Sausalito.

236

39 **S**ausalito has gotten more notoriety than it deserves since Sally Stanford made a bid for a council seat. Before winning an election, she had made an attempt each two years for ten years. One time, it was reported, she took out two sets of papers to cover the race two years ahead. "May as well save wear and tear," she said. One wonders if she was losing faith in herself or in the voters. During her first few attempts in the early '60s, there were only 1,800 registered voters, of whom less than a thousand voted. Elections were won on ten or twenty votes. Thirty was a mandate. The votes were split among a number of candidates. A fluke in the weather could swing an election, or something as small as a luncheon in a fine home, for the women invited took all morning to prepare themselves and all afternoon to recover. They didn't have time to vote.

Sally Stanford has had a life as varied as a protean and just as colorful. Being born in Baker, Oregon, gave her the incentive to leave and see the country. Her view of things was from a difficult angle in the beginning, but she must have had peripheral vision, for she soon saw that if she was going to get ahead, she'd have to be alert and take care of herself. There was another aspect too; she had just enough French in her blood to want to be called Madam and enough honesty to deserve it. So she started her own house of joy, and ran it on strict rules. She was a business woman who knew what she wanted and how to attain it. When she bought the old Valhalla in Sausalito and applied for a use permit to make a restaurant out of it, eyebrows in town got more stretching and exercise than ever before in history. There was no need to worry. She had proven that when the right person and principles are applied, the layaway plan can be used to good advantage. The success of the restaurant showed she was ready to try her hand at other things.

It seems that Sally Stanford always did things differently than most people, and coming to Sausalito to live is another example. Most residents chose the town to live in because it was attractive to them. Not Sally. For many years after opening the restaurant, she lived in San Francisco and only moved to Sausalito when she was forced to do so by election laws that required an applicant for city council be a resident. Her first attempt to be a councilwoman was a fiasco at the polls, but the public meetings provided her with the opportunity to speak her mind. She was humorous, although not clever; she offered great relief to an otherwise boring and repetitive evening; she was laughed at and with, but never taken seriously. Sally didn't learn much in the first two attempts and only her hangers-on voted for her. During the third attempt she had a platform, but forgot the foundation. Her proposals were good, but there was absolutely no way to implement them. It was grandiose finger-writing in the sky, looking good but fading quickly upon examination.

Perhaps her most serious proposal was to provide toilets for tourists. Everyone admitted it was a serious problem, but no one wanted to mention it publicly. Something like that would never bother Sally. In one of her lighter moments she may have figured it was one way of giving people relief without raising their taxes. It wasn't a bad idea.

After each election, she demanded, got, and paid for a recount of all ballots. There has never been a reversal, but it added a little anxiety to the final results, and kept her name before the public eye a little longer.

Sally stated that the only reason she lost the races was that she played fair and square but the 'hill' people used dirty tricks with last minute mailers for opposing candidates. "That isn't my game," she remarked, "and I'll never stoop to it." But there were more elections to come.

A few months after the 1964 election in which she was defeated, one councilman resigned and moved away. Because Sally had been the loser by only 30 votes, her backers demanded that she be appointed to fill the vacancy. On the night the announcement was to be made, city hall was filled. Sally spoke in her own behalf, others spoke for her. It looked good, publicly, for Sally, until Alan Bonapart spoke. In one of the shortest, most cogent speeches ever made in city hall, he said:

"Members of the council. In my understanding of the democratic process, it would be wrong to appoint Sally Stanford to the council. She has proven three times that she is not the people's choice, definitely not a winner, and there's no tradition in America that says you must appoint a loser."

So they didn't, and Sally had to wait until another election.

In 1966 she ran a professional-type campaign, with full page ads, bumper stickers, posters, signs, and several mailings to all constituents. Still she lost. She spent more money than all other candidates combined. She had another recount and vowed that the next time she'd show 'em. She almost did.

In 1968 there were five candidates for three seats; an able and dedicated incumbent, an energetic nurse with rather conservative tendencies, a carpenter with the opposite, and an artist who had run for a council seat more times than Sally.

Sally's strategy in 1968 ran the gamut of all known political tricks, plus a few of her own invention. She even resorted to the old axiom that says, 'people vote against politicians, not for them.' She introduced party politics for the first time in the city's history. But still she lost by 30 votes, the magical number.

Four times she had attempted to win in the only ways she knew how. First as a lark, then on humor, unreasonable and unworkable proposals, then with her own kind of sallies and slogans. But she did not convince a majority of voters of her ability, nor did she again in 1970. Her only chance to win would be longevity, a change in the composition of voters, and a lack of strong candidates. That combination came in 1972. Over the years, many dedicated old-timers had left town, some had died, and younger people, swingers, as they were often called, had moved in. They had no interest in city government, but thought that if Sally did, why not vote for her? "It would be fun," they said, or "It will shake up city hall." So Sally won and, at this writing, the foundation has withstood her mild vibrations.

Predicting how Sally will vote on an issue is a game many play during meetings. But there are no bets made when the question concerns a developer; on that issue she is consistent. 'Anything for development' seems to be her motto. It's a far cry from 1957, when she worked so hard to prevent development in front of her restaurant. It's a case of whose shore is boxed.

40 Sausalito is a happy town. It could hardly escape being so, considering the people who have lived there. Not all has been peace and cooperation over the years, but there's never been a rounded person who hasn't had a few square corners knocked off. Same with a town. City politics have been normal for a small town. There were factions within factions in various camps of the residents from time to time, which some say is a healthy sign. Only the businessmen have been in agreement on one thing: 'We must draw more tourists.' But they can never agree on how to do it. An exception to the call for more tourists came late in 1974 when the Golden Gate Bridge district decided to add new and larger ferries to the San Francisco-Sausalito run. These ferries, if operating at capacity, would spill nearly 10,000 passengers per day onto the

241

already crowded streets of Sausalito. With these figures in mind the business community met to discuss the proposed ferry terminal and the new ferries. Their conclusion came as a complete surprise to everyone. The Bridge district was expecting the merchants' backing. But no, they would oppose the new ferries. Their fear was that with that many people eager to make purchases, the quality of merchandise would diminish, and fast-service, junky, schlocky souvenir shops would take over and ruin the town. Short memories. They forgot whom they replaced. But having a stake in the town makes one proud and possessive.

From time to time citizens have fought against some of the proposals that they thought would change their town too much. Those protests were against the big and obvious and immediate plans, such as a development or re-routing of the main highway around the waterfront. In some protests they were successful, in others they were as ineffectual as pleading to an avalanche; it was too late; the snow and ice were tumbling down. Generally the outcome depended upon how much money and effort had been put into the project before it came to the attention of the citizens. As could be expected, those who protested were accused of being against progress. It was a charge they would happily serve time for if it would save their town.

Occasionally there was a low undercurrent of grumbling over the loss of resident-serving shops, with a few threats to elect new councilmen, but with each new election came promises. It was predictable. When people say they will do everything within their power to maintain the residential atmosphere, they could very well mean it. But they had to work within the framework of the free enterprise system. Anyone who wanted to sell wicker chickens or bottles melted into ash trays was guaranteed the right to try. The councilmen in the past cannot be wholly blamed. No public official was expected to be a prophet. If he were able to foretell the future

242

he could better spend his time than serving on the Sausalito city council. Most public officials in the early development of Sausalito only concerned themselves with alternatives to the problem before them. If a novel idea was presented it was put down with the phrase: 'A thing like that has never been done in Sausalito.' This attitude prompted the remark, "Their philosophy is stamped, 'Made by Readers Digest.' " A good example was the proposed library in the ferry. A plan such as that today would get careful consideration.

One important tool that present city officials use to great advantage, which past officials didn't have, is the right and the duty to consider whether large proposals are going to have a detrimental impact on the community, commonly known as the environmental impact review. Actually many citizens in the past were trying to tell the councilmen that 'we don't want a lot of people coming to Sausalito. It will change our town. We came here because we liked it as it is.' That's environmental impact. They were right, but ahead of their time. Taken as a whole, allowing Sausalito to become a shopping complex has so drastically changed the character of the town that a visitor from a few years back would be astonished over the transformation. This questionable progress has taken its toll, but in doing so it has sounded the alarm for the future. There has been progress of another kind since early 1970.

The recent councilmen and women aren't afraid to step on the toes of big business. It's refreshing to see city officials doing more than justifying their actions. Learning from the past and applying the lessons to the future is revolutionary. It's true they have stopped some proposals, all in the interest of attempting to keep Sausalito under strict control; something past councils were more lenient about. Some of the present council members lean heavily on the environmental concept, which is as lawfully open to them as applying for a business permit is open to others. But the council members

243

know that if left unchecked, the opportunists would overrun the town with high rise apartments and waterfront commercial developments. The accusation of being anti-business is a minor charge in a major cause. Sausalito is still a town and must be saved from being totally developed for its total business potential. There have been acquisitions of land for open space, all made with an uphill fight against developers. Open space is a previous commodity which once lost can never be regained. Developers have met their match. The arguments of sales tax dollars gained by additional commercial development no longer carry any weight. Sausalito has sales tax dollars. What it needs is room and fresh air so citizens can function in their town. With cars bumper to bumper for a mile on either end of the town on any normal day, why stretch it further? Sausalito is never going to be the quiet village it once was, but that is no reason to give up. Approving large developments will mean a tremendous impact on the town; rejecting them is a devastating impact on financial backers. Take your pick.

The mildest form of controversy arises when residents discuss the period when Sausalito changed, and as many say, 'became spoiled.' Some old timers say, 'The Golden Gate Bridge killed Sausalito.' Residents who came twenty years later say it was a great town then. 'What spoiled Sausalito was the Village Fair. It was an OK town 'til then, but now it's nothing but a nervous conspiracy.' One camp says the town has no spirit. 'Sure it's a carnival, but whoever heard of a carnival without children? There's nothing downtown for kids. All those vacationing celebrants give a false impression of gaiety. It's all a mask of merchandising, with money the only meaning.'

Perhaps the most inaccurate impression of Sausalito is held by a few short sighted merchants who said, 'Sausalito would be a dead town if it weren't for tourists.' That view could only be shared by those who believe the life blood of the community is commerce. It's true, that without tourism

244

the cash registers would die and the carnival-like spirit would succumb, but the town was active and alive before gift shops, as we hope these pages show.

Today there are many residents who say, 'Far out. It's a fun town. I wouldn't want to live anywhere else in the world.' And so it goes. With all the differences there is agreement on one point: Sausalito is no town for a hobby horse.

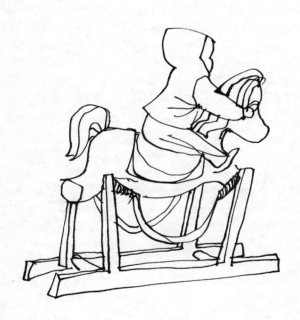

The author was deeply involved in the life of Sausalito for more than twenty years. He moved there in 1948, built a home in 1950, worked in a local hardware store and acted as handyman and general home problem-solver for a wide circle of friends. He served on the Community Appearances Advisory Board, the Planning Commission, and the City Council. In 1969, he and his wife regretfully moved to Alto, near Mill Valley, where he has a home inspection service. The reader will see where he left his heart.